Central & South
Africa

phrase book & dictionary

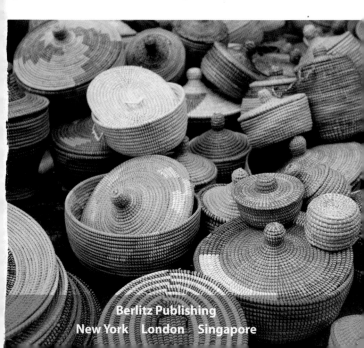

Berlitz Publishing
New York   London   Singapore

No part of this book may be reproduced, stored in a retrieval system or transmitted in any form or means electronic, mechanical, photocopying, recording or otherwise, without prior written permission from APA Publications.

Contacting the Editors
Every effort has been made to provide accurate information in this publication, but changes are inevitable. The publisher cannot be responsible for any resulting loss, inconvenience or injury. We would appreciate it if readers would call our attention to any errors or outdated information. We also welcome your suggestions; if you come across a relevant expression not in our phrase book, please contact us at: **comments@berlitzpublishing.com**

All Rights Reserved
© 2015 Berlitz Publishing/APA Publications (UK) Ltd.
Berlitz Trademark Reg. U.S. Patent Office and other countries. Marca Registrada. Used under license from Berlitz Investment Corporation.

First Printing: 2015
Printed in China

Senior Commissioning Editor: Kate Drynan
Translation: updated by Wordbank
Simplified phonetics: updated by Wordbank
Cover & Interior Design: Beverley Speight
Production Update: AM Services
Production Manager: Vicky Mullins
Picture Researcher: Tom Smyth (cover); Beverley Speight (interior)
Cover Photo: All iStockphoto except Ariadne Van Zandbergen beads and telephone sign

Interior Photos: All Ariadne Van Zandbergen except Beverley Speight 24, 41, 118, 161, 180, 218; Bigstockphoto p38; Yadid Levy 133, 171, 172, 209; Peter Stuckings 169; Anna Mockford & Nick Bonetti 160; David Dunai 41; SuperStock p206; iStockphoto 6, 32, 75, 121, 142, 144, 148, 176, 179, 192-201, 204

Contents

How to use this Book

Sometimes you see two alternatives separated by a slash. Choose the one that's right for your situation.

ESSENTIAL

I'm on vacation/
business.

I'm going to…
I'm staying at
the…Hotel.

Estou de férias/em negócios. *ee-stawoo deh feh-ree-uhz/eng neh-gaw-see-yooz*
Vou para… *vawoo puh-ruh…*
Permaneço no hotel… *pehr-muh-neh-soo noo aw-tehl…*

Words you may see are shown in YOU MAY SEE boxes.

YOU MAY SEE…

COUVERT

PREÇO-FIXO

EMENTA

cover charge

fixed-price

menu

Any of the words or phrases listed can be plugged into the sentence below.

Tickets

A(n)…ticket.
 one-way
 return-trip
 first-class

Um bilhete… *oong bee-lyeht…*
de ida *deh ee-thuh*
de ida e volta *deh ee-thuh ee vaul-tuh*
em primeira classe *eng pree-may-ruh klah-she*

Portuguese phrases appear in purple.

Read the simplified pronunciation as if it were English. For more on pronunciation, see page 8.

The Dating Game

Can I buy you a drink?
I'm not interested.

O que quer beber? *oo keh kehr ben·behr*
Não estou interessado m/interessada f.
nohm ee·stawoo een·treh·sah·thoo/
een·treh·sah·thuh

For Social Media, see page 24.

Related phrases can be found by going to the page number indicated.

When different gender forms apply, the masculine form is followed by *m*; feminine by *f*

The best way to get around Mozambique is to go by **chapas** (minibus) or **machibombas** (buses) in bigger towns. If you prefer to hire a car, a 4WD is best to access all areas and roads.

Information boxes contain relevant country, culture and language tips.

Expressions you may hear are shown in You May Hear boxes.

YOU MAY HEAR...

Como é ele/ela? *kau·moo eh ehleh/ehluh*

What does he/she look like?

Color-coded side bars identify each section of the book.

Portuguese

Essentials

Hello.	**Olá.** _aw_-lah
Goodbye.	**Adeus.** uh-_dehoosh_
Yes/No/OK	**Sim/Não/O.K.** seeng/nohm/aw-_kay_
Excuse me! (attention)	**Desculpe!** deh-_skoolp_
Excuse me. (to get past)	**Com licença.** kohng lee-_sehn_-suh
Sorry!	**Perdão!** pehr-_dohm_
I'd like something…	**Queria algo…** keh-_ree_-uh _ahl_-goo…
How much/many?	**Quanto/Quantos?** _kwuhn_-too/_kwuhn_-toos
And/or	**e/ou** ee/oo
Where is the…?	**Onde está…?** aund ee-_stah_…
My name is…	**Chamo-me… [Meu nome é…]** _shuh_-moo meh… [mehoo _nau_-mee eh…]
I'm going to…	**Vou para…** vauoo _puh_-ruh…
Please.	**Se faz favor [Por favor].** seh fahz _fuh_-vaur [poor _fuh_-vaur]
Thank you.	**Obrigado m/Obrigada f.** aw-bree-_gah_-doo/ aw-bree-_gah_-duh
You're welcome.	**De nada.** deh _nah_-duh
Could you speak more slowly?	**Pode falar mais devagar?** pawd fuh-_lahr_ meyez deh-vuh-_gahr_
Could you repeat that?	**Importa-se de repetir?** eeng-_pawr_-tuh-seh deh reh-peh-_teer_
I don't understand.	**Não compreendo.** nohm kaum-pree-_ehn_-doo
Do you speak English?	**Fala inglês?** _fah_-luh eng-_lehz_
I don't speak (much) Portuguese.	**Não falo (bem) português.** nohm _fah_-loo (beng) poor-too-_gehz_
Where are the restrooms [toilets]?	**Onde são as casas de banho [os banheiros]?** aund sohm uhz _kah_-zuhz deh _buh_-nyoo [ooz bah-_nyay_-rooz]
Help!	**Ajuda!** uh-_zsoo_-duh

You'll find the pronunciation of the Portuguese letters and words written in gray after each sentence to guide you. Simply pronounce these as if they were English, noting that any underlines indicate an additional emphasis or stress or a lengthening of a vowel sound. As you hear the language being spoken, you will quickly become accustomed to the local pronunciation and dialect.

Essentials

Numbers

0	**zero**	_zeh_•roo
1	**um** _m_/**uma** _f_	oong/_oo_•muh
2	**dois** _m_/**duas** _f_	doyz/_thoo_•uhz
3	**três**	trehz
4	**quatro**	_kwah_•troo
5	**cinco**	_seeng_•koo
6	**seis**	sayz
7	**sete**	seht
8	**oito**	_oy_•too

9	**nove** *nawv*
10	**dez** *dehz*
11	**onze** *aunz*
12	**doze** *dauz*
13	**treze** *trehz*
14	**catorze** *kuh·taurz*
15	**quinze** *keengz*
16	**dezasseis [dezesseis]** *dehz·eh·sayz*
17	**dezassete [dezessete]** *dehz·eh·seht*
18	**dezoito** *dehz·oy·too*
19	**dezanove [dezenove]** *deh·zuh·nawv*
20	**vinte** *veent*
21	**vinte e um** *m*/**uma** *f* *veent ee oong/oo·muh*
30	**trinta** *treeng·tuh*
40	**quarenta** *kwuh·rehn·tuh*

50	**cinquenta**	
	seeng·kwehn·tuh	
60	**sessenta**	
	seh·sehn·tuh	
70	**setenta**	
	seh·tehn·tuh	
80	**oitenta**	
	oy·tehn·tuh	
90	**noventa**	
	noo·vehn·tuh	
100	**cem**	
	sehn	
101	**cento e um** *m*/**uma** *f*	
	sehn·too ee oong/oo·muh	
200	**duzentos** *m*/**duzentas** *f*	
	doo·zehn·tooz/doo·zehn·tuhz	
500	**quinhentos** *m*/**quinhentas** *f*	
	kee·nyehn·tooz/kee·nyehn·tuhz	
1,000	**mil**	
	meel	
10,000	**dez mil**	
	dehz meel	
1,000,000	**um milhão**	
	oong mee·lyohm	

Time

What time is it?	**As horas, por favor?**
	uhz aw·ruhz poor fuh·vaur
It's noon [mid-day].	**É meio-dia.**
	eh may·oo dee·uh
Twenty past four	**Quatro e vinte.**
	kwah·troo ee veent

A quarter to nine.	**Um quarto para as nove.**
	oong kwahr•too puh•ruh uhz nawv
5:30 a.m./p.m.	**Cinco e meia de manhã/da tarde.**
	seeng•koo ee may•uh deh muh•nyuh/duh tahrd

Days

Monday	**segunda-feira**
	seh•goon•duh fay•ruh
Tuesday	**terça-feira**
	tehr•suh fay•ruh
Wednesday	**quarta-feira**
	kwahr•tuh fay•ruh
Thursday	**quinta-feira**
	keen•tuh fay•ruh
Friday	**sexta-feira**
	say•stuh fay•ruh
Saturday	**sábado**
	sah•buh•thoo
Sunday	**domingo**
	doo•meeng•goo

Portuguese is the official language spoken in Angola, Mozambique, Guinea-Bissau and Equatorial Guinea, as well as the islands of Cape Verde and São Tomé & Príncipe.

Dates

yesterday	**ontem**
	awn•teng
today	**hoje**
	auzseh
tomorrow	**amanhã**
	uh•muh•nuh
day	**o dia**
	oo dee•uh
week	**a semana**
	uh seh•muh•nuh
month	**o mês**
	oo mehz
year	**o ano**
	oo uh•noo
Happy New Year!	**Feliz Ano Novo!**
	feh•leez uh•noo noh•voh
Happy Birthday!	**Feliz Aniversário!**
	feh•leez uh•nee•vehr•sahr•ee•oo

Months

January	**Janeiro**
	zher•nay•roo
February	**Fevereiro**
	feh•vray•roo
March	**Março**
	mahr•soo
April	**Abril**
	uh•breel
May	**Maio**
	meye•oo

June	**Junho**	
	zsoo•nyoo	
July	**Julho**	
	zsoo•lyoo	
August	**Agosto**	
	uh•_gaus_•too	
September	**Setembro**	
	seh•_tehm_•broo	
October	**Outubro**	
	aw•_too_•broo	
November	**Novembro**	
	noo•_vehm_•broo	
December	**Dezembro**	
	deh•_zehm_•broo	

Arrival & Departure

I'm on vacation [holiday]/business.	**Estou de férias/em negócios.** ee•_stawoo_ deh _feh_•ree•uhz/eng neh•_gaw_•see•yooz
I'm going to…	**Vou para…** vawoo _puh_•ruh…
I'm staying at the… Hotel.	**Permaneço no hotel…** pehr•muh•_neh_•soo noo aw•_tehl_…

Flights operated by international airlines are the most reliable means of flying in and out of Africa. For travel to any of the islands, it is definitely easiest to arrive and depart on a pre-arranged package. There are connecting flights from Cape Verde and São Tomé & Príncipe to Angola and Ghana.

Money

Where's...?	**Onde é...?** _aund eh..._
the ATM	**o multibanco [a caixa automática]** _oo mool·tee·buhn·koo [uh keye·shuh aw·too·mah·tee·kuh]_
the bank	**o banco** _oo buhn·koo_
the currency exchange office	**o câmbio** _oo kuhm·bee·oo_
What time does the bank open/close?	**A que horas é que o banco abre/fecha?** _uh keh aw·ruhz eh keh oo buhn·koo ah·breh/feh·shuh_
I'd like to change dollars/pounds into euros/reais.	**Queria trocar dólares/libras em euros/reais.** _keh·ree·uh troo·kahr daw·luhrz/lee·bruhz eng ehoo·rooz/rree·eyez_
I want to cash some traveler's checks [cheques].	**Quero cobrar [trocar] cheques de viagem.** _keh·roo koo·brahr [troo·kahr] sheh·kehz deh vee·ah·zseng_
I'll pay...	**Pago...** _pah·goo..._
in cash	**com dinheiro** _kaum dee·nyay·roo_
by credit card	**com o cartão de crédito** _kaum oo kuhr·tohm deh kreh·dee·too_

For Numbers, see page 8.

YOU MAY SEE...

Each country has its own currency and changing money even in neighboring countries can be difficult if not impossible. Note that old, used and crumpled U.S. dollars are also difficult to change everywhere.

Getting Around

How do I get to the city center?	**Como é que vou para o centro da cidade?** _kau_•moo eh keh vawoo _puh_•ruh oo _sehn_•troo duh see•_dahd_
Where's…?	**Onde é…?** _aund eh_…
the airport	**o aeroporto** _oo uh•eh•rau•_paur_•too_
the train station [the railway station]	**a estação de caminho de ferro [a estação ferroviária]** _uh ee•stuh•_sohm_ deh kuh•_mee_•nyoo deh _feh_•rroo [uh ee•stuh•_sohm_ feh•rroo•vee•_ah_•ree•uh]_
the bus station	**a estação de camionetas [ônibus]** _uh ee•stuh•_sohm_ deh kah•meeoo•_neh_•tuhz [_aw_•nee•boos]_

15

The best way to get around Mozambique is to go by **chapas** (minibus) or **machibombas** (buses) in bigger towns. If you prefer to hire a car, a 4WD is best to access all areas and roads. Hitchhiking (for a small fee) is also common and sometimes the only means of independent travel but always travel in pairs and take the usual precautions.

How far is it?	**A que distância fica?** *uh keh dee-stuhn-see-uh fee-kuh*
Where can I buy tickets?	**Onde posso comprar bilhetes?** *aund paw-soo kaum-prahr bee-lyehtz*
A one-way/return-trip ticket to…	**Um bilhete de ida/de ida e volta para…** *oong bee-lyeht deh ee-thuh/deh ee-thuh ee vaul-tuh puh-ruh…*
How much?	**Quanto custa?** *kwuhn-too koo-stuh*
Which…?	**Qual…?** *kwahl…*
gate	**porta** *port-uh*
line	**linha** *lee-nyuh*
platform	**plataforma** *plah-tuh-fawr-muh*
Where can I get a taxi?	**Onde posso apanhar [pegar] um táxi?** *aund paw-soo uh-puh-nyar [peh-gahr] oong tahk-see*
Please take me to this address.	**Leve-me a esta morada [neste endereço].** *leh-veh-meh uh eh-stuh maw-rah-duh [nehst ehn-deh-reh-soo]*
To…Airport, please.	**Ao aeroporto de…, por favor.** *ahoo uh-eh-rau-paur-too deh…poor fuh-vaur*
I'm in a hurry.	**Estou com pressa.** *ee-stawoo kaum preh-suh*
Could I have a map?	**Pode dar-me um mapa?** *pawd dahr-meh oong mah-puh*

Driving in Angola is not recomended and car-jacking is a risk. Local bus services are usually the most reliable means of transportation here. That said, the roads are opening up and the routes between principal towns and cities are being improved.

Tickets

When's…to…?	**A que horas é…para…?**
	uh kee <u>aw</u>•ruhz eh…<u>puh</u>•ruh…
the (first) bus	**a (primeira) camioneta [o (primeiro) ônibus]**
	uh (pree•<u>may</u>•ruh) kah•meeoo•<u>neh</u>•tuh
	[oo (pree•<u>may</u>•roo) <u>aw</u>•nee•boos]
the (next) flight	**o (próximo) vôo** *oo (<u>praw</u>•see•moo) <u>vau</u>•oo*
the (last) train	**o (último) comboio [trem]**
	oo (<u>ool</u>•tee•moo) kaum•<u>baw</u>•eeoo [treng]
Where can I buy	**Onde posso comprar bilhetes?**
tickets?	*aund <u>paw</u>•soo kaum•<u>prahr</u> bee•<u>lyehtz</u>*
One/Two ticket(s),	**Um bilhete/Dois bilhetes, se faz favor.**
please.	*oong bee•<u>lyeht</u>/doyz bee•<u>lyehtz</u> seh fahz fuh•<u>vaur</u>*
For today/tomorrow.	**Para hoje/amanhã.** *puh•ruh auzseh/uh•muh•<u>nyuh</u>*
A(n)…ticket.	**Um bilhete…** *oong bee•<u>lyeht</u>…*
one-way	**de ida** *deh <u>ee</u>•thuh*
return-trip	**de ida e volta** *deh <u>ee</u>•thuh ee <u>vaul</u>•tuh*
first-class	**em primeira classe** *eng pree•<u>may</u>•ruh <u>klah</u>•she*

17

I have an e-ticket.	**Eu tenho um bilhete electrónico.** *ehoo teh•nyoo oong bee•lyeht ee•lek•tro•nee•kuh*
How long is the trip?	**Quanto tempo demora a viagem?** *kwuhn•too tehm•poo deh•maw•ruh uh vee•ah•zseng*
Is it a direct train?	**É um comboio directo?** *eh oong kaum•baw•eeoo dee•reh•too*
Could you tell me when to get off?	**Pode-me dizer quando eu devo sair?** *paw•deh meh dee•zehr kwuhn•doo deh•voo suh•eer*
Is this the bus to...?	**Este ônibus vai para ...?** *ehst aw•nee•boos vay parah ...*
I'd like to...my reservation.	**Queria...a minha reserva.** *keh•ree•uh...uh mee•nyuh reh•zehr•vuh*
cancel	**cancelar** *kuhn•seh•lahr*
change	**mudar** *moo•dahr*
confirm	**confirmar** *kaum•feer•mahr*

For Time, see page 10.

Car Hire

Where can I rent a car?	**Onde posso alugar um carro?** *aund paw•soo uh•loo•gahr oong kah•rroo*
I'd like to rent...	**Queria alugar...** *keh•ree•uh uh•loo•gahr...*
a cheap/small car	**um carro barato/pequeno** *oong kah•rroo buh•rah•too/peh•keh•noo*
a 2-/4-door car	**um carro de duas/quatro portas** *oong kah•rroo deh thoo•uhz/kwah•troo pawr•tuhz*
a(n) automatic/manual	**um carro automático/de mudanças** *oong kah•rroo awoo•too•mah•tee•koo/deh moo•thuhn•suhz*
a car with air conditioning	**um carro com ar condicionado** *oong kah•rroo kaum ahr kawn•dee•seeoo•nah•thoo*

YOU MAY HEAR...

sempre em frente *sehm•preh eng frehn•teh*	straight ahead
à esquerda *ah ee•skehr•duh*	on the left
à direita *ah dee•ray•tuh*	on the right
depois de/ao dobrar da esquina *deh•poyz deh/ahoo doo•brahr duh ees•kee•nuh*	on/around the corner
em frente de *eng frehn•teh deh*	opposite
por trás de *poor trahz deh*	behind
a seguir ao m/à f *uh seh•geer ahoo/ah*	next to
depois do m/da f *deh•poyz thoo/duh*	after
norte/sul *nawrt/sool*	north/south
leste/oeste *lehs•the/aw•ehs•teh*	east/west
no semáforo *noo seh•mah•fau•roo*	at the traffic light
no cruzamento *noo croo•zuh•mehn•too*	at the intersection

a car seat	**um assento de carro de bebé** oong uh‑*sehn*‑too deh *kah*‑rroo deh beh‑*beh*
How much…	**Quanto é…?** *kwuhn*‑too eh…
per day/week	**por dia/semana** poor *dee*‑uh/seh‑*muh*‑nuh
Are there any discounts?	**Há descontos?** ah dehs‑*kaum*‑tooz

Places to Stay

Can you recommend a hotel?	**Pode recomendar-me um hotel?** pawd reh‑kaw‑mehn‑*dahr*‑meh oong aw‑*tehl*
I have a reservation.	**Tenho uma reserva.** *teh*‑nyoo *oo*‑muh reh‑*zehr*‑vuh
My name is…	**Chamo-me… [Meu nome é…]** *shuh*‑moo‑meh… [mehoo *naum*‑eh eh…]
Do you have a room…?	**Tem um quarto…?** teng oong *kwahr*‑too…

There are breathtakingly beautiful island resorts in São Tomé & Príncipe and Cape Verde while in the towns and cities, there are boutique B&Bs, apartments to rent and hotels of all categories.

for one/two	**para um/dois** _puh_•ruh oong/doyz
with a bathroom	**com quarto de banho [banheiro]** kaum _kwahr_•too deh _buh_•nyoo buh•_nyay_•roo
with air conditioning	**com ar condicionado** kaum ar kawn•dee•seeoo•_nah_•thoo
For...	**Para...** _puh_•ruh...
tonight	**hoje à noite** auzseh _ah_ noyt
two nights	**duas noites** _thoo_•uhz noytz
one week	**uma semana** _oo_•muh seh•_muh_•nuh
How much is it?	**Quanto custa?** _kwuhn_•too _koo_•stuh
Do you have anything cheaper?	**Há mais barato?** ah meyez buh•_rah_•too
What time is check-out?	**A que horas temos de deixar o quarto?** uh kee _aw_•ruhz _teh_•mooz deh thay•_shahr_ oo _kwahr_•too
Can I leave this in the safe?	**Posso deixar isto no cofre?** _paw_•soo thay•_shahr_ ee•stoo noo _kaw_•freh
Can I leave my bags?	**Posso deixar a minha bagagem?** _paw_•soo day•_shahr_ uh _mee_•nyuh buh•_gah_•geng
Can I have the bill/ a receipt?	**Pode dar-me a conta/uma factura [um recibo]?** pawd _dahr_•meh uh _kaum_•tuh/_oo_•muh fah•_too_•ruh [oong reh•_see_•boo]
I'll pay in cash/by credit card.	**Pago com dinheiro/com o cartão de crédito.** _pah_•goo kaum dee•_nyay_•roo/kaum oo kuhr•_tohm_ deh _kreh_•dee•too

Communications

Where's an internet café?	**Onde fica um internet café?** aund _fee_•kuh oong een•tehr•_neht_ kuh•_feh_
Can I access the Internet here?	**Tenho acesso à internet aqui?** _teh_•nyoo uh•_seh_•soo ah een•tehr•_neht_ uh•_kee_

Can I check my e-mail here?	**Posso ler o meu e-mail aqui?** _paw_•soo lehr oo mehoo ee-_mehl_ uh-_khee_
How much per (half) hour?	**Quanto é por (meia) hora?** _kwuhn_•too eh poor (_may_•uh) _aw_•ruh
How do I connect/ log on?	**Como conecto/faço o logon?** _kau_•moo koo-_nehk_•too/_fah_•soo oo _law_•gawn
A phone card, please.	**Um credifone [cartão telefónico], se faz favor.** oong kreh•dee•_faun_ [kuhr-_tohm_ tehl•eh•_fawn_•ee•koo] seh fahz fuh•_vaur_
Can I have your phone number?	**Pode dar-me o seu número de telefone?** pawd _dahr_•meh oo sehoo _noo_•meh•roo deh tehl•_fawn_
Here's my number/ e-mail address.	**Este é o meu número/e-mail.** ehst eh oo mehoo _noo_•meh•roo/ee•_mehl_
Call me/Text me.	**Telefone-me/Manda-me uma mensagem de texto.** tehl•_fawn_•eh•meh/_muhn_•duh•meh _oo_•muh mehn•_sah_•zseng deh _tehk_•stoo
E-mail me.	**Envie-me um e-mail.** ehn•_vee_•eh meh oong ee•_mehl_
Hello. This is...	**Estou [Alô]. Fala...** ee•_stawoo_ [aw•_lah_]. _fah_•luh...
I'd like to speak to...	**Queria falar com...** keh•_ree_•uh fuh•_lahr_ kaum...

Could you repeat that, please?	**Importa-se de repetir, por favor?** *eem·pawr·tuh·seh deh reh·peh·teer poor fuh·vaur*
I'll call back later.	**Chamo mais tarde.** *shuh·moo meyez tahr·deh*
Bye.	**Adeus.** *uh·deeoosh*
Where's the post office?	**Onde são os correios?** *aund sohm ooz koo·rray·ooz*
I'd like to send this to...	**Gostaria de mandar isto para...** *goo·stuh·ree·uh deh muhn·dahr ee·stoo puh·ruh...*
Can I...?	**Posso...?** *paw·soo...*
access the internet	**aceder a internet** *uh·seh·dehr uh een·tehr·neht*
check e-mail	**ler o meu e-mail** *lehr oo mehoo ee·mehl*
print	**imprimir [impressar]** *eeng·pree·meer [eeng·preh·sahr]*
plug in/charge my laptop/iPhone/iPad/BlackBerry	**ligar/carregar o meu laptop/iPhone/iPad/Blackberry** *lee·gahr/kahr·reh·gahr oo mehoo laptop/iPhone/iPad/Blackberry*
What is the WiFi password?	**Qual é a senha do WiFi?** *kwahl eh uh seh·nyuh doo WiFi*
Is the WiFi free?	**O WiFi é grátis?** *oo WiFi eh grah teez*
Do you have bluetooth?	**Tem bluetooth?** *teng bluetooth*
Do you have a scanner?	**Tem um scanner?** *teng oong scanner*

Most hotels offer free WiFi or LAN internet connection. Be prepared for periods of poor to non-existant connections though, despite claims to the contrary.

Social Media

Are you on Facebook/Twitter?	**Está no Facebook/Twitter?** *ee·stah noo facebook/twitter*
What's your username?	**Qual é o seu nome de utilizador?** *kwahl eh oo sehoo naum·eh deh oo·tee·lee·zuh·daur*
I'll add you as a friend.	**Vou adicioná-lo como amigo.** *vawoo·oo uh·dee·seeoo·nah·loo kau·moo uh·mee·goo*
I'll follow you on Twitter.	**Vou segui-lo no Twitter.** *vawoo·oo seh·gee·loo noo Twitter*
Are you following…?	**Está a seguir…?** *ee·stah uh seh·geer…*
I'll put the pictures on Facebook/Twitter.	**Vou colocar as fotos no Facebook/Twitter.** *vawoo koo·loo·khahr uhz faw·tawz noo Facebook/Twitter*
I'll tag you in the pictures.	**Vou identificá-lo nas fotos.** *vawoo ee·dehnt·tee·fee·kah·loo nuhz faw·tawz.*

Conversation

Hello.	**Olá.** *aw·lah*
How are you?	**Como está?** *kau·moo ee·stah*
Fine, thanks.	**Bem, obrigado** *m*/**obrigada** *f.* behm *aw·bree·gah·doo/aw·bree·gah·duh*

Excuse me! (to get attention)	**Desculpe!** *dehz•kool•peh*
Do you speak English?	**Fala inglês?** *fah•luh eeng•lehz*
What's your name?	**Como se chama?** *kau•moo seh shuh•muh*
My name is…	**Chamo-me… [Meu nome é…]** *shuh•moo meh… [mehoo naum•ee eh…]*
Nice to meet you.	**Muito prazer.** *mooee•too pruh•zehr*
Where are you from?	**De onde é?** *deh aund eh*
I'm from the U.S./U.K.	**Sou dos Estados Unidos/da Inglaterra.** *soh dooz ee•stah•dooz oo•nee•dooz/duh eeng•luh•teh•rruh*
What do you do?	**O que é que faz?** *oo kee eh keh fahz*
I work for…	**Trabalho para…** *truh•bah•lyoo puh•ruh…*
I'm a student.	**Sou estudante.** *sauoo ee•stoo•duhnt*
I'm retired.	**Sou reformado** *m***/reformada** *f* **[aposentado** *m***/aposentada** *f***].** *soh reh•foor•mah•thoo/reh•foor•mah•thuh [uh•poo•zehn•tah•doo/uh•poo•zehn•tah•duh]*

25

Romance

Would you like to go out for a drink/dinner?	**Queres ir tomar uma bebida/comer fóra?** _keh_•rehz eer too•_mahr_ oo•muh beh•_bee_•thuh/ _koo_•mehr _faw_•ruh
What are your plans for tonight/tomorrow?	**Quais são os seus planos para hoje à noite/ amanhã?** kweyez sohm ooz sehooz _pluh_•nooz _puh_•ruh auzseh ah noyt/uh•muh•_nyuh_
Can I have your number?	**Podes dar-me o teu número de telefone?** _pawd_•ehz _dahr_•meh oo tehoo _noo_•meh•roo deh tehl•_fawn_
Can I join you?	**Posso acompanhar-te?** _paw_•soo uh•kaum•puh•_nyahr_•teh
Can I buy you a drink?	**O que quer beber?** oo keh kehr beh•_behr_
I love you.	**Amo-te [Te amo].** _uh_•moo teh [teh _uh_•moo]

Accepting & Rejecting

I'd love to.	**Adorava [adoraria] ir.** uh·daw·*rah*·vuh [uh·doo·ruh·*ree*·uh] eer
Where should we meet?	**Onde nos vamos encontrar?** aund nooz *vuh*·mooz ehng·kaun·*trahr*
I'll meet you at the bar/your hotel.	**Vou ter contigo [te encontrar] ao bar/hotel.** vauoo tehr kaun·*tee*·goo [tee ehn·kaun·*trahr*] ahoo bahr/*aw*·tehl
I'll come by at...	**Eu passo por lá às...** ehoo *pah*·soo poor lah ahz...
What's your address?	**Qual é a sua morada [endereço]?** kwahl eh uh *soo*·uh maw·*rah*·duh [ehn·deh·*reh*·soo]
I'm busy.	**Mas tenho imenso [muito] que fazer.** muhz *teh*·nyoo ee·*mehn*·soo [*mooee*·too] keh fuh·*zehr*
I'm not interested.	**Não estou interessado *m*/interessada *f*.** nohm ee·*stawoo* een·treh·*sah*·thoo/een·treh·*sah*·thuh
Leave me alone.	**Deixe-me em paz.** *day*·sheh· meh eng pahz
Stop bothering me!	**Está quieto!** ee·*stah* kee·*eh*·too

27

Food & Drink

Eating Out

Can you recommend a good restaurant/bar?	**Pode recomendar-me um bom restaurante/bar?** *pawd reh·kaw·mehn·dahr·meh oong bohng reh·stahoo·ruhnt/bar*
Is there a(n) traditional Portuguese/ inexpensive restaurant near here?	**Há um restaurante tradicional português/ barato perto daqui?** *ah oong reh·stuhoo·ruhnt truh·dee·see·oo·nahl por·too·gehz/buh·rah·too pehr·too duh·kee*
A table for…, please.	**Uma mesa para…, se faz favor.** *oo·muh meh·zuh puh·ruh…seh fahz fuh·vaur*
Could we sit…?	**Podemos sentar-nos…?** *poo·deh·mooz sehn·tahr·nooz…*
here/there	**aqui/ali** *uh·kee/uh·lee*
outside	**lá fora** *lah faw·ruh*
in a non-smoking area	**na área para não-fumadores [não-fumantes]** *nuh ah·ree·uh puh·ruh nohmfoo·muh·daur·ehs [nohmfoo·muhnts]*
I'm waiting for someone.	**Estou à espera de alguém.** *ee·stawoo ah ee·speh·ruh deh ahl·gehm*
Where's the restroom [toilet]?	**Onde são as casas de banho [os banheiros]?** *aund sohmuhz kah·zuhz deh buh·nyoo [ooz buh·nyay·rooz]*
A menu, please.	**Uma ementa, por favor.** *oo·muh ee·mehn·tuh poor fuh·vaur*
What do you recommend?	**O que é que me recomenda?** *oo keh eh keh meh reh·koo·mehn·duh*

I'd like…	**Queria…** *keh·ree·uh…*	
Some more…, please.	**Mais…, se faz favor.** *meyez…seh fahz fuh·vaur*	
Enjoy your meal.	**Bom apetite.** *bohng uh·peh·tee·teh*	
The check [bill], please.	**A conta, por favor.** *uh kaum·tuh poor fuh·vaur*	
Is service included?	**O serviço está incluído?** *oo sehr·vee·soo ee·stah een·kloo·ee·thoo*	
Can I pay by credit card?	**Posso pagar com cartão de crédito?** *paw·soo puh·gahr kaumkuhr·tohm deh kreh·dee·too*	
Could I have a receipt, please?	**Pode darme uma factura [um recibo], por favor?** *pawd dahr·meh oo·muh fah·too·ruh [oong reh·see·boo] poor fuh·vaur*	

YOU MAY SEE…

COUVERT	cover charge
PREÇO-FIXO	fixed-price
EMENTA	menu
UMA EMENTA DO DIA	menu of the day
SERVIÇO (NÃO) INCLUÍDO	service (not) included
ESPECIAIS	specials

Breakfast

as carnes frias *uhz kahr·nehz free·uhz*	cold cuts
o doce de fruta [geleia] *oo dau·seh deh froo·tuh [zseh·lay·uh]*	jam
a manteiga *uh muhn·tay·guh*	butter

a omelete	omelet
uh aw•meh•leh•tuh	
o ovo…	…egg
oo au•voo…	
muito fervido/fervido macio	hard-boiled/
mooee•too fehr•vee•thoo/fehr•vee•thoo	soft-boiled
muh•see•oo	
estrelado [frito]	fried
ee•struh•lah•doo [free•too]	
mexido	scrambled
meh•shee•doo	
o pão	bread
oo pohm	
o queijo	cheese
oo kay•zsoo	
as salsichas	sausages
uhz sahl•see•shuhz	
as torradas	toast
uhz too•rrah•duhz	
o toucinho	bacon
oo tau•see•nyoo	
o yogurte	yogurt
oo yaw•goort	

Appetizers

a sopa à pescador	fish soup
uh sau•puh ah pehs•kuh•daur	
a sopa transmontana	vegetable soup with bacon
a sau•puh truhnz•moo•tuh•nuh	and bread
a sopa canja	chicken and rice soup
keng•zsuh	

a sopa de tomate   tomato soup
a <u>sau</u>·puh deh too·<u>maht</u>

o paio   smoked pork fillet
oo <u>peye</u>·oo

Meat

o bife [filete]   steak
oo bee**f** [fee·<u>leh</u>·chee]

o borrego [carneiro]   lamb
oo boo·<u>rreh</u>·goo [kuhr·<u>nay</u>·roo]

a carne de porco   pork
uh kahrn deh <u>paur</u>·koo

a carne de vaca   beef
uh kahrn deh <u>vah</u>·kuh

o frango   chicken
oo <u>fruhn</u>·goo

a vitela   veal
uh vee·<u>tehl</u>·uh

YOU MAY HEAR...

mal passado *m*/passada *f*   rare
mahl puh·<u>sah</u>·thoo/puh·<u>sah</u>·thuh

meio passado *m*/passada *f*   medium
<u>may</u>·oo puh·<u>sah</u>·thoo/puh·<u>sah</u>·thuh

bem passado *m*/passada *f*   well-done
beng puh·<u>sah</u>·thoo/puh·<u>sah</u>·thuh

Fish & Seafood

o bacalhau	cod
oo buh•kuh•lyahoo	
as almôndegas	fishballs
uhz ahl•mawn•deh•guhz	
o arenque	herring
oo uh•rehn•keh	
a lagosta	lobster
uh luh•gau•stuh	
o salmão (fumado) [defumado]	(smoked) salmon
oo suh•mohm (foo•mah•thoo) [deh•foo•mah•do]	
os camarões	shrimp [prawns]
ooz kuh•muh•roings	

Vegetables

as batatas	potatoes
uhz buh•tah•tuhz	
as cebolas	onions
uhz seh•bau•luhz	
a cenoura	carrot
uh seh•nau•ruh	

os cogumelos	mushrooms
ooz koo·goo·<u>meh</u>·looz	
a couve	cabbage
uh <u>kaw</u>·veh	
as ervilhas	peas
uhz eer·<u>vee</u>·lyuhz	
as favas	broad beans
uhz <u>fah</u>·vuhz	
o feijão	kidney beans
oo fay·<u>zsohm</u>	
o tomate	tomato
oo too·<u>maht</u>	

Sauces & Condiments

o sal	salt
o sahl	
a pimenta	pepper
uh pee·<u>mehn</u>·tuh	
mostarda	mustard
mooz·tahr·duh	
ketchup	ketchup
ketchup	

While tuna and other fish is popular in Guinea, Cape Verde, Mozambique and São Tomé & Príncipe, grains and yams, sweet potatoes and other vegetables often form the basis of stews and other hearty dishes.

Fruit & Dessert

a banana *uh buh·<u>nuh</u>·nuh*	banana
a laranja *uh luh·<u>ruhn</u>·zsuh*	orange
o limão *oo lee·<u>mohm</u>*	lemon
a maçã *uh muh·<u>suh</u>*	apple
os morangos *ooz moo·<u>ruhn</u>·gooz*	strawberries
a pêra *uh <u>peh</u>·ruh*	pear
o gelado *oo zseh·<u>lah</u>·thoo*	ice cream
o chocolate *oo shoo·koo·<u>laht</u>*	chocolate
a baunilha *uh bahoo·<u>nee</u>·lyuh*	vanilla
a tarte *uh tahrt*	tart
a mousse *uh <u>moo</u>·seh*	mousse
o creme leite *oo krehm layt*	custard

Drinks

The wine list/drink menu, please. **A carta dos vinhos/ementa de bebidas, se faz favor.** *uh <u>kahr</u>·tuh dooz <u>vee</u>·nyooz/ee·<u>mehn</u>·tuh deh beh·<u>bee</u>·duhz seh fahz fuh·<u>vaur</u>*

What do you recommend?	**O que é que me recomenda?** *oo keh eh keh meh reh·koo·mehn·duh*
I'd like a bottle/glass of red/white wine.	**Queria uma garrafa/um copo de vinho tinto/branco.** *keh·ree·uh oo·muh guh·rrah·fuh/oong kaw·poo deh vee·nyoo teen·too/bruhn·koo*
The house wine, please.	**O vinho da casa, se faz favor.** *oo vee·nyoo duh kah·zuh seh fahz fuh·vaur*
Another bottle/glass, please.	**Outra garrafa/Outro copo, se faz favor.** *auoo·truh guh·rrah·fuh/auoo·troo kaw·poo ser fahz fuh·vaur*
I'd like a local beer.	**Gostaria uma cerveja local.** *goo·stuh·ree·uh oo·muh sehr·vay·zsuh loo·kahl*
Can I buy you a drink?	**Posso oferecer-lhe uma bebida?** *paw·soo aw·freh·sehr·lyeh oo·muh beh·bee·thuh*
Cheers!	**Viva!** *vee·vuh*
A coffee/tea, please.	**Um café/chá, se faz favor.** *oong kuh·feh/shah seh fahz fuh·vaur*
Black.	**Bica [Cafezinho].** *bee·kuh [kuh·feh·zee·nyoo]*
With...	**com...** *kaum...*
milk	**leite** *layt*
sugar	**açúcar** *uh·soo·kuhr*
artificial sweetener	**adoçante** *uh·doo·suhnty*
A..., please.	**..., se faz favor.** *...seh fahz fuh·vaur*
juice	**Um sumo [suco]** *oong soo·moo [soo·koo]*
soda	**Um refresco** *oong reh·freh·skoo*
sparkling/still water	**Uma água com/sem gás** *oo·muh ah·gwuh kaum/sehmgahz*
Is the tap water safe to drink?	**A água da torneira é boa para beber?** *uh ah·gwuh duh toor·nay·ruh eh baw·uh puh·ruh beh·behr*

Leisure Time

Sightseeing

Where's the tourist office?	**Onde é o posto de turismo [informações turísticas]?** *aund eh oo <u>pau</u>•stoo deh too•<u>reez</u>•moo [een•foor•muh•<u>soings</u> too•<u>ree</u>•stee•kuhz]*
What are the main points of interest?	**O que há de mais interessante para se ver?** *oo kee ah deh meyez een•tehr•reh•<u>suhnt</u> <u>puh</u>•ruh seh vehr*
Do you have tours in English?	**Tem excursões em inglês?** *teng ee•skoor•<u>soings</u> eng eng•<u>lehz</u>*
Can I have a map/guide?	**Pode dar-me um mapa/guia?** *pawd <u>dahr</u>•meh oong <u>mah</u>•puh/gee•uh*

Shopping

Where is the market/mall [shopping?	**Onde é o mercado/o centro comercial?** *aund eh oo mehr•<u>kah</u>•thoo/oo <u>sehn</u>•troo koo•mehr•see•<u>ahl</u>*
I'm just looking.	**Estou só a ver [vendo].** *ee•<u>stawoo</u> saw uh vehr [<u>vehn</u>•doo]*
Can you help me?	**Pode ajudar-me?** *pawd uh•zsoo•<u>dahr</u>•meh*
I'm being helped.	**Alguém está a [me] ajudar-me.** *ahl•<u>gehng</u> ee•<u>stah</u> uh [meh] uh•zsoo•<u>dahr</u>•meh*

How much is it?	**Quanto é?** _kwuhn•too eh_
I'd like …	**Queria…** _keh•<u>ree</u>•uh…_
That one, please.	**Aquele _m_/Aquela _f_, por favor.** _uh•<u>kehl</u>/uh•<u>keh</u>•luh poor fuh•<u>vaur</u>_
That's all, thanks.	**É tudo, obrigado _m_/obrigada _f_.** _eh <u>too</u>•doo aw•bree•<u>gah</u>•doo/aw•bree•<u>gah</u>•thuh_
Where can I pay?	**Onde pago?** _aund <u>pah</u>•goo_
I'll pay in cash/ by credit card.	**Pago com dinheiro/com o cartão de crédito.** _<u>pah</u>•goo kaum dee•<u>nyay</u>•roo/kaum oo kuhr•<u>tohm</u> deh <u>kreh</u>•dee•too_
A receipt, please.	**Um recibo, se faz favor.** _oong reh•<u>see</u>•boo seh fahz fuh•<u>vaur</u>_

YOU MAY SEE…

aberto/fechado	open/closed
entrada/saída	entrance/exit

Sport & Leisure

When's the game?	**Quando é o jogo?** _kwuhn•doo eh o <u>zsau</u>•goo_
Where's…?	**Onde é…?** _aund eh…_
the beach	**a praia** _uh <u>preye</u>•uh_
the park	**o parque** _oo <u>pahr</u>•keh_
the pool	**a piscina** _uh pee•<u>see</u>•nuh_
Is it safe to swim here?	**Pode-se nadar aqui sem perigo?** _pawd seh nuh•<u>dah</u> uh•<u>kee</u> sehn peh•<u>ree</u>•goo_
Can I hire golf clubs?	**Posso alugar tacos?** _<u>paw</u>•soo uh•loo•<u>gahr</u> <u>tah</u>•kooz_
How much per hour?	**Qual é a tarifa por hora?** _kwahl eh uh tuh•<u>ree</u>•fuh poor <u>aw</u>•ruh_
How far is it to…?	**A que distância fica…?** _uh keh dee•<u>stuhn</u>•see•uh <u>fee</u>•kuh…_
Can you show me on the map?	**Pode indicar-me no mapa?** _pawd een•dee•<u>kahr</u>•meh noo <u>mah</u>•puh_

Going Out

What is there to do in the evenings?	**O que há para se fazer à noite?** *oo keh ah* <u>puh</u>*•ruh seh fuh•*<u>zehr</u> *ah noyt*
Do you have a program of events?	**Tem um programa dos espectáculos?** *teng oong proo•*<u>gruh</u>*•muh dooz ee•spehk•*<u>tah</u>*•koo•looz*
What's playing at the movies [cinema] tonight?	**O que há no cinema hoje à noite?** *oo kee ah noo see•*<u>neh</u>*•muh auzseh ah noyt*
Where's...?	**Onde é...?** *aund eh...*
the downtown area	**o centro** *oo* <u>sehn</u>*•troo*
the bar	**o bar** *oo bar*
the dance club	**a discoteca** *uh deez•koo•*<u>teh</u>*•kuh*
Is there a cover charge?	**É preciso pagar entrada [ingresso]?** *eh preh•*<u>see</u>*•zoo puh•*<u>gahr</u> *ehn•*<u>trah</u>*•duh [een•*<u>greh</u>*•soo]*
Is this area safe at night?	**Esta zona é segura à noite?** *eh•stuh zau•nuh eh seh•goo•ruh ah noyt?*

For the adventurous, the crystal clear waters encourage snorkeling and diving while windsurfing and kitesurfing will suit the more active visitor. Alternatively, boat trips, dhow safaris and even hiking are ways to get out and about and get active. Check what is available in the area and book through a reputable tour operator.

Baby Essentials

Do you have...?	**Tem...?** _teng..._
a baby bottle	**um biberom** _oong bee-<u>brohng</u>_
baby wipes	**os toalhetes de limpeza para o bebé [nenê]** _ooz too-ah-<u>lyehtz</u> deh leem-<u>peh</u>-zuh <u>puh</u>-ruh oo beh-<u>beh</u> [neh-<u>neh</u>]_
a car seat	**um assento de carro** _oong uh-<u>sehn</u>-too deh <u>kah</u>-rroo_
a children's menu/ portion	**uma ementa/dose [porção] de criança** _oo-muh ee-<u>mehn</u>-tuh/<u>daw</u>-zeh [poor-<u>sohm</u>] deh kree-<u>uhn</u>-suh_
a child's seat	**uma cadeirinha de criança** _<u>oo</u>-muh kuh-day-<u>ree</u>-nyuh deh kree-<u>uhn</u>-suh_
a crib	**uma cama de bebé [neném]** _<u>oo</u>-muh <u>kuh</u>-muh deh beh-<u>beh</u> [neh-<u>neh</u>]_
diapers [nappies]	**as fraldas** _uhz <u>frahl</u>-duhz_
formula	**fórmula de bebé [neném]** _<u>fawr</u>-moo-luh deh beh-<u>beh</u> [neh-<u>neh</u>]_
a pacifier [dummy]	**uma chupeta** _<u>oo</u>-muh shoo-<u>peh</u>-tuh_
a playpen	**um parque para crianças** _oong pahr-<u>kuh</u> puh-ruh kree-<u>uhn</u>-suhz_
a stroller [pushchair]	**uma cadeira de bebé [neném]** _<u>oo</u>-muh kuh-day-<u>ruh</u> deh beh-<u>beh</u> [neh-<u>neh</u>]_
Can I breastfeed the baby here?	**Posso amamentar o bebé [neném] aqui?** _<u>paw</u>-soo uh-muh-mehn-<u>tahr</u> oo beh-<u>beh</u> [neh-<u>neh</u>] uh-<u>kee</u>_
Where can I change the baby?	**Onde posso mudar o bebé [neném]?** _aund <u>paw</u>-soo moo-<u>thahr</u> oo beh-<u>beh</u> [neh-<u>neh</u>]_

Disabled Travelers

Is there...?	**Há...?** *ah...*
access for the disabled	**acesso para deficientes físicos** *uh·seh·soo puh·ruh deh·fee·see·ehntz fee·see·kooz*
a wheelchair ramp	**uma rampa de cadeira de rodas** *oo·muh ruhm·puh deh kuh·day·ruh deh raw·thuhz*
a handicapped-[disabled-] accessible toilet	**uma casa de banho acessível para deficientes** *oo·muh kah·zuh deh buh·nyoo uh·seh·see·vehl puh·ruh deh·fee·see·ehntz*
I need...	**Preciso de...** *preh·see·zoo deh...*
assistance	**assistência** *uh·see·stehn·see·uh*
an elevator [lift]	**um elevador** *oong eh·leh·vuh·daur*
a ground-floor room	**um quarto no primeiro andar** *oong kwahr·too noo pree·may·roo uhn·dahr*
Please speak louder.	**Por favor, fale mais alto.** *poor fuh·vaur fah·leh mey·ez ahl·too*

Health & Emergencies

Emergencies

Help!	**Socorro!** soo-_kau_-rroo
Go away!	**Vá-se embora!** _vah_-seh ehng-_baw_-ruh
Call the police!	**Chame a polícia!** _shuh_-meh uh poo-_lee_-see-uh
Stop thief!	**Pára ladrão!** _pah_-ruh luh-_drohm_
Get a doctor!	**Chame um médico!** _shuh_-meh oong _meh_-dee-koo
Fire!	**Fogo!** _fau_-goo
I'm lost.	**Estou perdido** _m_/**perdida** _f._ ee-_stawoo_ pehr-_dee_-thoo/pehr-_dee_-thuh
Can you help me?	**Pode ajudar-me?** pawd uh-zsoo-_dahr_-meh
Call the police!	**Chame a polícia!** _shuh_-meh uh poo-_lee_-see-uh
Where's the police station?	**Onde é a esquadra [delegacia] da polícia?** aund eh uh ee-_skwahr_-duh [deh-leh-guh-_see_-uh] thuh poo-_lee_-see-uh
My son/daughter is missing.	**O meu filho/A minha filha desapareceu.** oo mehoo _fee_-lyoo/uh _mee_-nyuh _fee_-lyuh deh-zuh-puh-ruh-_seoo_

Health

I'm sick [ill].	**Estou doente.** ee-_stawoo_ doo-_ehnt_
I need an English-speaking doctor.	**Preciso de um médico que fale inglês.** preh-_see_-zoo deh oong _meh_-dee-koo keh _fah_-leh eeng-_lehz_
It hurts here.	**Dói-me aqui.** _doy_-meh uh-_kee_

On arrival at your destination, check with your hotel for the local emergency numbers to have to hand in case you need them.

YOU MAY HEAR...

Preencha este formulário.
pree·eng·sheh eh·stuh fawr·muh·lah·reeoo

Fill out this form.

A sua identificação, por favor. *uh soo·uh
ee·dehnt·tee·fee·kuh·sohm por fuh·vaur*

Your identification, please.

Quando/Onde é que foi? *kwuhn·doo/
aund eh keh foy*

When/Where did it happen?

Como é ele/ela? *kau·moo eh ehleh/ehluh*

What does he/she look like?

Where's the pharmacy [chemist]?	**Onde fica a farmácia?** *aund fee·kuh uh fuhr·mah·see·uh*
I'm (not) pregnant.	**(Não) Estou grávida.** *(nohm) ee·stawoo grah·vee·thuh*
I'm allergic to antibiotics/penicillin.	**Sou alérgico m/alérgica f a antibióticos/penicilina.** *sawoo uh·lehr·gee·koo/uh·lehr·gee·kuh uh uhn·tee·bee·aw·tee·kuhz/peh·neh·seh·lee·nuh*
I'm on...	**Estou em...** *ee·stawoo eng...*

Dictionary

adaptor o adaptador
American o americano, a americana
and e
antiseptic cream a pomada
   antiséptica
aspirin a aspirina
at least pelo menos
athletics atletismo
attack o ataque
attendant o empregado,
   a empregada
attractive atraente
aunt a tia
baby o bebé [neném]
backpack a mochila
bad mau, má
bandage a ligadura [a atadura]
battle site o campo de batalha
beige beige [bege]
bikini o bikini [o biquini]
bird o pássaro
black preto
blue azul
bottle opener o abre-garrafas
   [o abridor de garrafas]
bowl a malga
boy o rapaz
boyfriend o namorado
bra o sutiã

bread o pão (escuro/integral)
   bread (brown/whole wheat)
bread roll o pãozinho
British britânico
brown o castanho
burger o hambúrguer
camera a máquina fotográfica
can opener o abre-latas [o abridor
   de latas]
cat o gato [a gata]
castle o castelo
cigarette o cigarro
cold frio; ~ (illness) a constipação
   [o resfriado]
comb o pente
computer o computador
condom o preservativo
contact lens as lentes de
   contacto
corkscrew o saca-rolhas
cup a chávena
dangerous perigoso
deodorant o desodorizante
   [o desodorante]
diabetic o diabético
dog o cão
doll a boneca
economy class a classe
   económica

electricity a electricidade
embassy a embaixada
Europe a Europa
except excepto
excess o excesso
exchange *v* trocar
exchange rate a taxa de câmbio
excursion a excursão
excuse me (apology) desculpe-me; **(to get attention)** desculpe
fly *v* voar
fork (utensil) o garfo
girl a menina
girlfriend a namorada
glass (drinking) o copo
glass (material) o vidro
good bom [boa]; ~ **morning** bom dia; ~**night** boa noite
gray o cinzento
green o verde
hairbrush a escova de cabelo; ~**spray** a laca para o cabelo
horse o cavalo
hot (temperature) quente; **(spicy)** picante
husband o marido
ice o gelo
icy *adj* gelado, gelada
I'd like… Queria…

insect repellent o repelente de insectos
Irish irlandês
jeans as calças de ganga
knife faca
lactose intolerant intolerantes à lactose
large grande
lentils as lentilhas
lighter o isqueiro
lotion a loção
love (a person) amar; **(a thing)** gostar de
matches (fire) os fósforos
medium (size) médio; **(cooked)** meio-passado
museum o museu
nail file lima para unhas
napkin o guardanapo
nurse o enfermeiro, a enfermeira
or ou
orange (fruit) a laranja; **(color)** cor-de-laranja
park o parque
partner o companheiro, a companheira
pen a caneta
pink cor-de-rosa
plate o prato
purple roxo

pyjama o pijama
rain v chover
raincoat a gabardine
razor a navalha;
~ **blade** a lâmina de barbear
red vermelho, vermelha
rice o arroz
salty salgado
sandals as sandálias
sanitary napkin o penso higiénico
[a toalha higiénica]
scissors a tesoura
shampoo o shampoo
[o xampu]
shoe o sapato
small pequeno m/ pequena f
sneakers as sapatilhas [os ténis]
snow a neve; v nevar
soap o sabonete
sock a peúga, meia [meia
curta]
spicy picante
spider a aranha
spoon a colher
stamp o selo
suitcase a mala de viagem
sun o sol
sunglasses os óculos de sol
sweatshirt a sweatshirt
[blusa de moleton]
swimsuit o fato [maiô] de banho

tampons os tampões higiénicos
ticket o bilhete; ~ **machine** a
máquina de venda de bilhetes;
~ **office** a bilheteira
[a bilheteria]
tie (clothing) a gravata
tissue o lenço de papel
toilet paper o papel higiénico
toothbrush a escova de dentes
toothpaste a pasta de dentes
toy o brinquedo
traffic o trânsito; ~ **jam**
o engarrafamento; ~ **circle**
a rotunda; ~ **light** o semáforo
trail o caminho; ~ **map** o mapa
train o comboio [o trem];
~ **station** a estação de caminho de
ferro [a estação ferroviária]
transfer (plane, train) o transbordo
translate v traduzir
trash o lixo; ~ **can** a lixeira
travel v viajar;
~ **agency** a agência de viagens
traveler's check o cheque de
viagens
T-shirt a T-Shirt [a camiseta]
underwear a roupa interior
vegan vegan
vegetarian vegetariano
walking route o itinerário a pé
wall a parede

wallet a carteira (de documentos)

warm *adj* morno, morna;
  v aquecer

wash *v* lavar

washing machine a máquina de
  lavar

watch *n* o relógio; *v* ver

water a água

water skis os skis aquáticos
  [os esquis-aquáticos]

weather o tempo; ~ **forecast**
  a previsão do tempo

wedding o casamento; ~ **ring**
  a aliança

white branco, branca

wife a mulher [a esposa]

with com

without sem

yam o inhame

year o ano

yellow amarelo, amarela

zoo o jardim zoológico, o zoo

Tswana

Essentials

Hello/Hi. (one person)	**Dumela.**
	Doo•meh•lah
Hello/Hi.	**Dumelang.**
(2 or more persons)	*doo•me•lah•ng*
Goodbye.	**Sala sentle.** *Sah•lah se•n•tl•eh*
Yes/No/OK.	**Ee/Nnyaa/Go siame.** *go•sea•ah•meh*
Excuse me!	**Tshwarelo!** *tsh•waa•reh•loh*
(to get attention)	
Excuse me.	**Tshwarelo!** *tshwaa•reh•loh*
(to get past)	
I'm sorry.	**Ke maswabi.** *ke•mar•swah•bee*
I'd like…	**Ke batla…** *ke•bar•tla*
How much?	**Ke bokae?** *key•boh•qae*
And/or.	**Le/kgotsa.** *leh/kgo•ts•ah*
Please.	**Tsweetswee.** *ts•we•ts•we*
Thank you.	**Ke a leboga.** *ke•ah•leh•bo•gah*
You're welcome.	**Go leboga nna.** *go•leh•bo•gah•nna*
Where's…?	**…kae?** *kar•eh*
I'm going to…	**Ke ya kwa…** *ke yah q•waa …*
My name is…	**Leina la me ke…** *lee•nah lah meh ke*
Please speak slowly.	**Ke kopa o bue ka iketlo tsweetswee.** *key•qo•par*
	o boo•eh qa ee•keh•tlo tswe•tswe
Can you repeat that?	**Ke kopa o boeletse seo?**
	key qo•par o bore•eh•lets•eh se•oh?
I don't understand.	**Ga ke tlhaloganye.**
	ga ke tlha•lo•ga•nye
Do you speak English?	**A o bua English?**
	ah oh boo•ah English

I don't speak (much) Tswana.	**Ga ke bue Tswana (ga kalo).**
	ga ke boo·eh Tuh·swah·nah gaa qa·loh
Where's the restroom [toilet]?	**Ntlwana e kwa kae?** *n·tlwaa·nah eh*
	k·waa qa·eh
Help!	**Ke kopa thuso!** *key qo·par two·sow*

You'll find the pronunciation of the Tswana letters and words written in gray after each sentence to guide you. Simply pronounce these as if they were English. As you hear the language being spoken, you will quickly become accustomed to the local pronunciation and dialect.

Numbers

0	**lefela** *le·fhe·lah*
1	**nngwe** *nn·gwe*
2	**pedi** *pair·dee*
3	**tharo** *tar·row*
4	**nne** *n·ne*
5	**tlhano** *tlhah·no*
6	**thataro** *tar·tar·row*
7	**supa** *su·pa*
8	**robedi** *row·bear·dee*
9	**robonngwe** *row·bow·n·gwe*
10	**lesome** *le·sow·meh*
11	**lesome le bongwe** *leh·sow·meh leh bongw·eh*
12	**lesome le bobedi** *leh·sow·mehleh boh·bedee*
13	**lesome le boraro** *leh·sow·meh leh bo·ra·row*

14	**lesome le bone** *leh•sow•meh leh boneh*
15	**lesome le botlhano** *leh•sow•meh leh botl•ha•no*
16	**lesome le borataro** *leh•sow•meh leh bo•ra•tar•row*
17	**lesome le bosupa** *leh•sow•meh leh bo•super*
18	**lesome le borobedi** *leh•sow•meh leh bo•row•bear•dee*
19	**lesome le borobonngwe** *leh•sow•meh leh bo•row•bow•n•n•gwe*
20	**masomeamabedi** *mah•sow•meh•ah•mar•bear•dee*
21	**masomeamabedi le bongwe** *mah•sow•meh•ah•mar•bear•dee•n•n•gwe*
30	**masomeamararo** *mah•sow•meh•ah•mar•rah•row*
40	**masomeamane** *mah•sow•meh•ah•mar•neh*
50	**masomeamatlhano** *mah•sow•meh•ah•mar•tl•ha•no*
60	**masomeamarataro** *mah•sow•meh•ah•mar•rah•tar•row*
70	**masomeasupa** *mah•sow•meh•ah•super*
80	**masomearobedi** *mah•sow•meh•ah•row•bear•dee*
90	**masomearobonngwe** *mah•sow•meh•ah•row•bow•n•n•gwe*
100	**lekgolo** *leh•kgo•loh*
101	**lekgolo le bongwe** *eh•kgo•low leh bo•ngwe*
200	**makgolo a mabedi** *ma•kgo•low ah mar•beh•dee*
500	**makgolo a matlhano** *ma•kgo•low ah mar•tl•hah•no*
1,000	**sekete** *circuit•eh*
10,000	**dikete tse some** *dee•cat•tea tse sow•meh*
1,000,000	**milione** *mee•lee•or•neh*

Time

What time is it?	**Ke nako mang?** *ke nah•core mar•ng*
It's midday.	**Ke sethoboloko.** *ke se•tow•boar•loh•core*
Five past three.	**Metsotso e metlhano morago ga ura ya boraro.** *metsore•tsore eh meh•tlha•no mow•rah•go ga oo•rah ya bow•rah•row*
A quarter to ten.	**Metsotso e le lesome le botlhano pele ga ura ya lesome.** *metsore•tsore eh le•sow•meh leh bo•tlhah•no pe•leh ga oo•rah ya leh•sow•meh*
5:30 a.m./p.m.	**5:30 phakela/maitseboa** *park•eh•laa)/mar•ee•tsee•bow•ah*

Days

Monday	**Mosupologo** *mow•sue•po•logo*
Tuesday	**Labobedi** *lah•bo•beh•dee*
Wednesday	**Laboraro** *lah•bo•rah•row*
Thursday	**Labone** *lah•bo•neh*
Friday	**Labotlhano** *lah•bo•tlha•no*
Saturday	**Matlhatso** *mar•tlha•ts•oh*
Sunday	**Sontaga** *so•n•tar•gg•ah*

Dates

yesterday	**maabane** *mar•ah•bar•neh*
today	**gompieno** *go•m•pee•eh•no*
tomorrow	**kamoso** *kar•mow•sow*
day	**letsatsi** *le•tsar•tsee*
week	**beke** *bear•keh*
month	**kgwedi** *kgwe•dee*
year	**ngwaga** *n•gwaa•gah*

Tswana is the official language of Botswana. There are approximately six million speakers of the language. English is also widely spoken.

| Happy New Year! | **Itumelele Ngwaga o Mosha!** *e•two•meh•leh•leh n•gwaa•gah oh mo•shar* |
| Happy Birthday! | **Itumelele Letsatsi la Botsalo!** *e•two•meh•leh•leh leh•tsa•tsee lah bo•tsar•low* |

Months

January	**Firikgong** *fee•ree•kgoh•ng*
February	**Tlhakole** *tlhaa•core•leh*
March	**Mopitlwe** *mow•pee•tlweh*
April	**Moranang** *mow•run•ah•ng*
May	**Motsheganong** *mow•tshe•gah•no•ng*
June	**Seetebosigo** *sir•et•ee•boh•sea•go*
July	**Phukwi** *poo•q•wee*
August	**Phatwe** *part•were*
September	**Lwetse** *l•were•ts•eh*
October	**Phalane** *par•llah•neh*
November	**Ngwanatsele** *ngwa•nah•tse•leh*
December	**Sedimonthole** *sir•dee•mow•n•to•leh*

Arrival & Departure

I'm on vacation [holiday]/business.	**Ke mo malatsing a boikhutso/kgwebo.** *ke more ma•lah•tsee•ng ah boo•ee•coo•tsoh*
I'm going to...	**Ke ya kwa...** *ke yah q•waa*
I'm staying at the...Hotel.	**Ke nna kwa Hoteleng.** *ke n•nah q•waa hot•air•leh•ng*

Money

Where's...?	...kae? *kar·eh*
the ATM	**ATM e kae?** *eh kar·eh*
the bank	**banka e kae?** *bar·n·kar·eh·kar·eh*
the currency exchange office	**ofisi ya kananyo ya madi e kae?** *oh·fee·see yah kah·na·nyo ya mar·dee eh·kar·eh*
When does the bank open/close?	**Banka e bulwa/tswalwa leng?** *bar·n·kar eh boo·lwer/tswa·lwer le·ng*
I'd like to change dollars/pounds sterling/euros into Pula.	**Ke batla go ananya didolara/diponto/diyuro mo Pula.** *key bar·t·lah go ana·ny·ah dee·door·lah·rah/ dee·po·n·toh/dee·you·row poo·lah*
I'd like to cash traveler's cheques.	**Ke batla go fetolela ditšheke tsa mosepele go nna madi a seatleng.** *ke bar·t·lah go fat·ow·leh·lah dee·cheque tsa moss·air·pe·leh go n·na mar·dee a·a se·ah·tle·ng*
Can I pay in cash?	**A nka duela ka madi a seatleng?** *ah n·kar doo·er·lah kar mar·dee a·a se·ah·tle·ng*
Can I pay by (credit) card?	**A nka duela ka karata (ya sekoloto)?** *ah n·car doo·er·lah kar karrat·ah (yar seh·ko·lo·to)*

For Numbers, see page 50.

YOU MAY SEE...

The currency is the **Botswana Pula (P)**, which is divided into 100 **thebe (t)**.
Coins: P1, P2, P5, 5t, 10t, 25t, 50t
Bills: P10, P20, P50, P100, P200

Getting Around

How do I get to town?	**Ke ya jang kwa toropong?** *ke yah jar•ng q•wa tow•row•pong*
Where's…?	**…kae?** *kar•eh*
the airport	**boemelafofane (bo kae?)** *(bo•air•meh•laf•fo•far•neh (bo kar•eh)*
the train station	**seteishene sa terena (se kae?)** *station sah te•reh•nah se kar•eh*
the bus station	**seteishene sa bese (se kae?)** *station sah bess se kar•eh*
Is it far from here?	**A go kgakala go tswa fa?** *ah go kga•kar•lah go tswa fa*
Where do I buy a ticket?	**Ke reka thekete kwa kae?** *ke reh•kar ticket q•waa kar•eh)*
A one-way/ return-trip ticket to…	**Thekete ya leeto la go ya/leeto la go ya le go boa go ya kwa…** *ticket yah le•air•tow le la go yah/le•air•tow lah go ya le go boar kwa*
How much?	**Ke bokae?** *ke bow•kar•eh*
Which gate/line?	**Mo hekeng efe/moleng ofe?** *more hair•care•ng efe/more•leh•ng oh•fe*
Which platform?	**Mo polatefomong efe?** *more plat•form•efe*

55

Where can I get a taxi? **Nka bona kae thekesi?**
n•kar•boh•nah kar•eh tax•ee

Take me to **Nkise kwa atereseng e.**
this address. *n•ki•seh q•waa address•eng eh*

To...Airport, please. **Kwa Boemelafofane jwa ..., tsweetswee.**
q•waa boar•air•meh•lah•fo•far•neh jua ..., tswe•tswe

I'm in a rush. **Ke itlhaganetse** *ke ee•tlh•aga•neh•tse*

Can I have a map? **Ke kopa mmapa** *ke ko•par•maa•par*

When driving around Botswana, bear in mind that if you need
to open a gate to get through, always remember to close it again
behind you. This is often to keep livestock in and wild animals out (or
vice versa!).

Tickets

When's...to Gaborone?	**...go ya kwa Gabarone ke leng?** *go ya q•waa Ga•bo•rone ke leh•n*
the (first) bus/	**bese (ya ntlha)** *bess yah n•tl•hah*
the (next) flight/	**sefofane (se se latelang)** *seh•fo•far•neh seh seh lah•te•lah•n*
the (last) train	**terena (ya bofelo)** *te•renah yah•bow•fair•lo*
One/Two ticket(s) please.	**Ke kopa thekete e le Nngwe/dithekete tse pedi tsweetswee.** *ke ko•par ticket e•le•nngwe/dee•ticket tse pair•dee tswe•tswe*
For today/tomorrow.	**Ya gompieno/kamoso** *yah go•m•pee•eh•no/kah•mo•soh*

A…ticket.	**thekete ya …** *ticket yah*
one-way	**leeto le le lengwe** *le·air·tow le le le·ngwe*
return trip	**leeto la go ya le go boa** *le·air·tow la go ya le go boar*
first class	**ya maemo a ntlha** *yah mar·eh·more a n·tlha*
I have an e-ticket.	**Ke na le thekete e e rekilweng ka inthanete.** *key nah le ticket e e rare·key·lwe·ng kar internet*
How long is the trip?	**Leeto le tsaya nako e e kae?** *le·air·tow le tsar·yah nah·kore e e car·eh*
Is it a direct train?	**A ke terena ya tlhamalalo?** *(ah key tey·reh·nah yah tlha·mar·lah·low)*
Is this the bus to…?	**A ke bese e e yang kwa…?** *ah ke bess e e yang q·waa*
Can you tell me when to get off?	**Ke kopa o mpolelele gore ke fologa leng.** *ke ko·par o m·paw·leh·leh go·reh ke fo·lo·ga leng*
I'd like to… my reservation.	**Ke batla go… peeletsomanno ya me.** *key bar·tla go peer·leh·tso·mar·nno yah meh*
cancel	**phimola** *pee·more·lah*
change	**fetola** *fe·to·lah*
confirm	**tlhomamisa** *tlho·mar·mee·sah*

For Time, see page 52.

Car Hire

Where's the car hire?	**Lefelo la phiriso yla dikoloi le kae?** *le·fe·low lahpee·ree·soh yah dee·kore·low·ee le kare·eh*
I'd like…	**Ke batla** *ke ba·tlah*
a cheap/small car	**koloi e e tlhotlhwatlase/e nnye** *kore·low·ee e e tlho·tlhwa·tla·seh*
an automatic/	**ya othomethiki** *yah automati·qi*
a manual	**manyuale** *many·ual*
air conditioning	**e e nang le tekanyetsomowa** *e e nah·n leh teh·car·n·yeh·tso·more·wah*

a car seat	**setulo sa koloi**
	sir•two•low sa kore•low•ee
How much…?	**Ke bokae…?** *keh bo kar•eh*
per day/week	**ka letsatsi/ka beke**
	kar le•tsa•tsee/kah bear•keh
Are there any	**A go na le diphokoletsotlhotlhwa?** *ah go nah leh*
discounts?	*dee•paw•core•leh•tso•tlho•tlhwa*

YOU MAY HEAR...

kwa pele ka tlhamalalo	straight ahead
q•waa peel•eh kar tlha•mar•lah•low	
molema *mo•leh•mar*	left
moja *mo•jar*	right
mo khoneng *more corne•ng*	around the corner
go lebagana le *go leh•bar•ga•nah le*	opposite
mo morago ga *mo more•rah•go gah*	behind
go bapa le (gaufi le) *go bar•par le*	next to
(ga•oo•fee leh)	
morago *moh•rah•go*	after
bokone/borwa *bow•kore•neh/bo•rwa*	north/south
botlhaba/bophirima *bore•tlha•ba/*	east/west
bore•pee•ree•mar	
kwa robotong *kwah ro•bore•tong*	at the traffic light
kwa makopanelong a ditsela	at the intersection
q•waa mar•core•par•neh•long ah di•tse•lah	

Places to Stay

Can you recommend a hotel?	**A go na le ho·te·le e o ka e buelelang**	*ah go na le ho·te·le e o ka e bue·le·la·ng*
I made a reservation.	**Ke dirile peeletso**	*ke dee·ree·leh pair·leh·tso*
My name is…	**Leina la me ke…**	*lee·nah lah meh ke*
Do you have a room…?	**A lo na le phaposi …?**	*ah lo nah le par·poo·sea*
for one/two	**ya motho a le mongwe/batho ba babedi**	*yah more·to ah leh more·ngwe/bar·two bar le bar·bear·dee*
with a bathroom	**e e nang le phaposi ya botlhapelo**	*e e nah·ng le par·poo·sea yah bore·tlha·pair·lo*
with air conditioning	**e e nang le tekanyetsomowa**	*e e nah·ng le te·kar·nye·tso·more·wah*
For…	**ya**	*yah*
tonight	**bosigo jo**	*bore·sea·go joh*
two nights	**masigo a mabedi**	*mar·sea·go ah·mar·bear·dee*
one week	**beke e le nngwe**	*bear·ke e le nn·gwe*
How much?	**Ke bokae?**	*ke bore·kah·eh*
Is there anything cheaper?	**A go na le sengwe se se tlhotlhwatlase?**	*ah go nah le se·ngwe se se tlho·tlhwa·tla·se*
When's checkout?	**Nako ya go tsamaya ke leng?**	*nah·kore yah go tsa·mar·yah ke·leng)*
Can I leave this in the safe?	**A nka tlogela se mo seifing?**	*ah n·kar tlo·ge·lah se moh safe·ing*
Can I leave my bags?	**A nka tlogela dikgetse tsa me?**	*ah n·car tlo·ge·la dee·kge·tsee tsa meh*
Can I have my bill/ a receipt?	**Ke kopa bili ya me/rasiti?**	*key ko·par bill·ee yah meh/rar·sea·tee*
I'll pay in cash/ by credit card.	**Ke tlaa duela ka madi a seatleng/ka karata ya sekoloto.**	*ke tlaa doo·eh·lah kar mar·dee a se·ah·tle·ng/kah kar·ah·tah yah sek·oh·lo·toh*

Communications

Where's an internet cafe?	**Lefelotiriso la inthanete le kae?** *le•fe•loh•tea•ree•soh la internet le ka•eh*
Can I access the internet/check my email?	**A nka bula inthanete/nka tlhola imeile ya me?** *ah n•car boo•lah Internet/n•nkar tlho•lah email yah meh)*
How much per half hour/hour?	**Ke bokae ka halofo ya ura/ura?** *ke bore•ka•eh ka ha•lo•foh yah•oo•rah*
How do I connect/ log on?	**Ke golagana jang/tsena jang?** *ke go•lah•ga•nah jar•ng/tse•nah jar•ng*
A phone card, please.	**Ke kopa karata ya founu, tsweetswee.** *ke ko•par karrat•ah yah phone, tswe•tswe*
Can I have your phone number?	**Ke kopa nomoro ya gago ya mogala.** *key ko•par no•more•row yah ga•go yah mo•ga•lah*
Here's my number/ email.	**Nomoro ya me ke e/imeile ya me ke imeile.** *no•more• row yah meh ke email*
Call me/text me.	**Nteletsa/nthomelele molaetsa** *n•te•leh•tsa/n•tow•meh•leh•leh more•lie•tsa*
I'll text you.	**Ke tlaa go romelela molaetsa** *ke tlaa go raw•meh•leh•lah more•lie•tsa*
Email me.	**Nthomelele imeile** *n•tow•meh•leh•leh email*
Hello. This is…	**Dumela. Se ke…** *doo•meh•lah. se ke*
Can I speak to…?	**Ke kopa go bua le …** *ke ko•par go boo•ah leh*
Can you repeat that?	**Ke kopa o boeletse seo?** *ke ko•par o bore•eh•leh•tse se•o*
I'll call back later.	**Ke tlaa letsa moragonyana.** *ke tlaa leh•tsa more•rar•go•nyana*
Bye.	**Sala sentle.** *sala se•n•tle*
Where's the post office?	**Poso e kwa kae?** *po•sow e q•waa kar•eh*

I'd like to send this to…	**Ke batla go romela se kwa go…** *key bar•tlaa go row•meh•lah se q•waa go*
Can I…?	**A nka…?** *ah n•ka*
access the internet	**bula inthanete** *boo•lah internet*
check my email	**tlhola imeile ya me** *tlho•lah email yah meh*
print	**gatisa** *gaa•tea•sah*
plug in/charge my laptop/iPhone/iPad/BlackBerry?	**polaka/tšhaja lepothopo ya me/iPhone/iPad/Blackberry?** *po•lah•kar/char•jar laptop yah meh/iPhone/iPad/BlackBerry*
access Skype?	**bula Skype?** *boo•lah Skype*
What is the WiFi password?	**Khunololamoraba ya WiFi ke mang?** *coo•no•lo•lah•mow•rubber ya WiFi ke mar•ng*
Is the WiFi free?	**A WiFi ke mahala?** *ah WiFi ke•mar•ha•lah*
Do you have bluetooth?	**A o na le bluetooth?** *(ah o nah leh•bluetooth)*
Do you have a scanner?	**A o na le sekenara?** *ah o nah leh scanner*

When you meet someone new, it is good manners and a sign of respect to shake hands and also to clasp the arm of the person's hand whom you are shaking with your other hand at the same time.

Social Media

Are you on Facebook/ Twitter?	**A o mo Facebook/Twitter?** *ah o mow Facebook/ Twitter*
What's your username?	**Leinatiriso la gago ke mang?** *lee·nah·tea·ree·soh lah ga·go ke mar·ng*
I'll add you as a friend.	**Ke tlaa go tsenya jaaka tsala.** *ke tlaa go tse·n·yah jar·ah·ka tsa·lah*
I'll follow you on Twitter.	**Ke tlaa go latela mo Twitter.** *ke tlaa go lah·te·lah mow Twitter*
Are you following…?	**A o latela…?** *ah o lah·te·lah*
I'll put the pictures on Facebook/Twitter.	**Ke tlaa baya ditshwantsho mo Facebook/Twitter.** *ke tlaa bar·yah dee·tshwa·n·tsho mow Facebook/ Twitter*
I'll tag you in the pictures.	**Ke tlaa go tag mo ditshwantshong.** *ke tlaa go tag mow dee·tshwa·n·tsho·ng*

Conversation

Hello/Hi. (one person)	**Dumela.** *Doo·meh·lah*
Hello/Hi. (2 or more persons)	**Dumelang.** *doo·me·lah·ng*
How are you?	**Le kae?** *le ka·eh*
Fine, thanks.	**Ke tsogile sentle, ke a leboga.** *ke tso·gi·le se·ntleh, ke ah leh·bow·ga*

Excuse me!	**Tshwarelo!**
	tshwa•reh•low
Do you speak English?	**A o bua English?**
	ah o boo•ah English
What's your name?	**Leina la gago ke mang?** *lee•nah la ga•go ke mar•ng*
My name is…	**Leina la me ke…** *lee•nah lah meh ke*
Nice to meet you.	**Ke itumeletse go kopana le wena.**
	ke e•two•meh•leh•tse go core•par•nah le were•nah
Where are you from?	**O tswa kwa kae?**
	o tswa q•waa ka•eh
I'm from the U.K./U.S.	**Ke tswa kwa U.K./U.S.**
	ke tswa•q•waa UK/U.S.
What do you do	**Tiro ya gago ke eng?**
for a living?	*tea•row yah ga•g ke eng*
I work for…	**Ke direla…**
	ke dee•reh•lah
I'm a student.	**Ke moithuti.**
	ke mow•ee•two•tea
I'm retired.	**Ke rotse tiro.** *ke row•tse tea•row*

Romance

Would you like to go out for a drink/dinner?	**A o ka rata go tswa o ya go nwa senotsididi/go ja dijo tsa maitseboa?** *ah o ka ra•ta go•tswa o yah go nwah se•no•tsee•dee•dee/go jar dee•jor tsa mar•ee•tsee•boar*
What are your plans for tonight/tomorrow?	**O rulagantse jang mo bosigong jo/kamoso?** *o roo•lah•gan•tse jar•ng mow bore•sea•go•ng jor/ka•mo•so*
Can I have your (phone) number?	**Ke kopa nomoro ya gago (ya mogala)?** *ke ko•par no•more•row yah ga•go (yah more•ga•la)*
Can I join you?	**Ke kopa go dula le wena?** *ke ko•par go doo•lah le were•nah*
Can I buy you a drink?	**Ke kopa go go rekela senotsididi?** *ke ko•par go go reck•elah se•no•tsee•dee•dee*
I love you.	**Ke a go rata.** *ke are go rah•ta*

Accepting & Rejecting

I'd love to.	**Nka rata.** *n•car rah•tar*
Where should we meet?	**Re kopane kae?** *reh tkoh•par•neh ka•eh*
I'll meet you at the bar/your hotel.	**Ke tlaa kopana le wena kwa bareng/kwa hoteleng ya gago.** *ke tlaa ko•par•nah leh were•nah q•waa bar•reng/q•waa ho•te•leng yah ga•go*
I'll come by at…	**Ke tlaa tla ka…** *ketlaa tla ka …*
I'm busy.	**Ke tshwaregile.** *ke tshwa•reh•gee•leh*
I'm not interested.	**Ga ke na kgatlhego.** *ga ke nah kga•tlhe•go*
Leave me alone.	**Tswa mo go nna.** *tswaa mow go n•na*
Stop bothering me!	**Tlogela go ntshwenya!** *tlo•ge•la go n•tshwe•n•yah*

Food & Drink

Eating Out

Can you recommend a good restaurant/ bar?	**A o ka buelela resetšhurente/bara e e siameng?** *Ah o kar boo•e•lelah restaurant/bar•ah e e sea•ah•meh•ng*
Is there a traditional/ an inexpensive restaurant nearby?	**A go na le resetšhurente ya setso/e e tlhotlhwatlase gaufinyana?** *ah go na le restaurant yah seh•tso/e e tlho•tlhwa•tlaa•seh ga•uu•fee•n•yana*
A table for…, please.	**Ke kopa tafole ya…, tsweetswee.** *ke core•par tar• for•leh yah … tswe tswe*
Can we sit…?	**A re ka nna …?** *ah reh ka nnah…*
here/there	**fa/fale** *far/far•leh*
outside	**kwa ntle** *q•waa n•tle*
in a non-smoking area	**mo lefelong le go sa gogelweng motsoko mo go lone** *mow leh•fe•long le go sa goh•ge•lweng mo go law•neh*
I'm waiting for someone.	**Ke emetse mongwe.** *ke air•meh•tse mow•ngwe*
Where are the toilets?	**Matlwana a kae?** *mar•tlwa•nah a ka•eh*
The menu, please.	**Ke kopa menyu, tsweetswee.** *ke core•par menu, ts•were ts•were*
What do you recommend?	**O buelela eng?** *o boo•ele•la e•ng*
I'd like…	**Ke batla …** *key bar•tlaa …*
Some more…, please.	**Ke kopa gape …, tsweetswee.** *key ko•par ga• per…, tswe•tswe*
Enjoy your meal!	**Itumelele dijo tsa gago!** *ee•two•meh•leh•leh dee•jor tsa ga•go*

The check [bill], please.	**Ke kopa bili, tsweetswee.**
	ke core·par bill·ee, tswe·tswe
Is service included?	**A tirelo e akareditswe?** *ah tea·reh·low e ark·ah·reh·dee·tswe)*
Can I pay by credit card/have a receipt?	**A nka duela ka karata ya sekoloto/Ke kopa rasiti?**
	ah n·ka doo·ch·lah ka ka·ra·ta ya se·ko·lo·toke ko·par rah·sea·tee

YOU MAY SEE…

TEFELO YA TSHIRELETSO	cover charge
TLHOTLHWA E E TLHOMAMENG	fixed price
MENYU (WA LETSATSI)	menu (of the day)
TIRELO (GA E A AKAREDIWA)	service (not) included
DITLHOTLHWATLASE	specials

Breakfast

bacon	**beikhone** *bacon*
bread	**borotho** *bore·raw·tore*
butter	**botoro** *bore·tore·raw*
cold cuts	**ditoki tsa coldmeat** *dee·to·ki tsa coldmeat*
cheese	**tšhise** *cheese*
…egg	**lee le le…** *leh·er le le*
hard/soft boiled	**bedisitsweng le le thata/boleta** *be·dee·sea·tswe·ng le le tar·tah/bo·letter*
fried	**le le gadikilweng** *le le ga·dee·kee·lweng*
scrambled	**le le fuduilweng** *leh leh foo·doo·ee·lweng*
jam/jelly	**jeme/jeli** *jam/jelly*
oatmeal [porridge]	**bogobe** *bo·go·be*
toast	**thouste** *toast*

| sausage | **soseije (bôrôsô)** *bore•row•sore* |
| yogurt | **yokate** *yo•ka•te* |

Appetizers

Fish soup	**sopo ya tlhapi** *sore•pore yah tlhaa•pea*
Vegetable/	**sopo ya merogo/tamati** *sore•pore yah meh•raw•go/*
tomato soup	*tar•mar•tea*
Chicken soup	**sopo ya koko** *sore•pore yah ko•ko*
Salad	**salate** *sa•late*

Meat

beef	**nama** *nar•mah*
chicken	**koko** *ko•ko*
lamb	**nama ya nku** *nar•mah yah n•coo*
pork	**nama ya kolobe** *nar•mah yah core•low•bear*
steak	**seteiki** *se•take*
veal	**nama ya namane** *nar•mah yah nar•mah•neh*
goat	**podi** *po•dee*

Fish & Seafood

Cod	**cod**
Fishcakes	**dikuku tsa tlhapi** *(di•fishkheike) (dee•koo•koo tsa tlha•pea)*
Herring	**herring**

YOU MAY HEAR...

...tala *tar•lah*	rare
...fa gare *far•ga•reh*	medium
...butswileng *boo•tswee•leng*	well-done

lobster	**lobesetara** *(lobster)*
salmons	**disalemone** *(dee·sah·leh·more·neh)*
Shrimp [prawns]	**disherimpi** *(dee·shrimp·ee)*

Vegetables

Beans	**dinawa** *dee·nar·wah*
Cabbage	**khabetšhe** *kha·be·che*
Carrots	**digwete** *dee·gweteh*
Mushroom	**mmasherumu** *ma·sh·e·roomoo*
Onion	**anyanese** *ah·nja·ne·se*
Peas	**dierekisi** *dee·air·reh·kiss·eh*
Potato	**tapole** *ta·pow·leh*
Tomato	**tamati** *tar·mar·tea*

Sauces & Condiments

Salt	**letswai** *leh·tswa·ee*
Pepper	**pepere** *peh·peh·reh*
Mustard	**mmasetete** *mma·seuteh·teh*
Ketchup	**tamatisousu** *tar·mar·tea·sow·sue*

Typical dishes in Botswana consist of meat and maize. The national dish is called **Seswaa** – a meat stew served with polenta. Grains, peas and pulses are popular as they are grown locally (you'll often see maize served at breakfast – **bogobe**), as are meat barbecues. Expect to discover many chicken, beef and goat dishes too.

Fruit & Dessert

apple	**apole** *ah·poh·leh*
banana	**panana** *pa·na·na*
lemon	**surunamune** *sue·rhoo·nar·mune*
orange	**namune** *nar·mune*
pear	**pere** *pear·e*
strawberries	**diseterooberi** *dee·straw·berry*
ice cream	**aesekherime** *eyes·cream*
chocolate/vanilla	**tšhokolete/vanilla** *chocolate/vanilla*
tart/cake	**terete/kuku** *teh·ret/coo·coo*
mousse	**mmuse** *moo·se*
custard/cream	**khasetete/kherime** *cars·tet/care·ream*

69

Drinks

The wine list/drink menu, please.	**Ke kopa lenaane la dibeine/menyu wa dino, tsweetswee.** *key core·par leh·naah·neh la dee·bear·ee·ne/meny wah dee·no*
What do you recommend?	**O buelela eng?** *o boo·ele·lah e·ng*
I'd like a bottle/glass of red/white wine.	**Ke kopa lebotlolo/galase ya beine e khibidu/tshweu.** *ke ko·pah leh·bore·tlo·loh/ga·lah·se yah bear·ee·ne e key·bea·doo/tshwe·uuu*

The house wine, please.	**Ke kopa beine e e leng teng, tsweetswee.** *ke ko•pah bear•ee•neh e e leng teng, tswe•tswe*
Another bottle/glass, please.	**Ke kopa lebotlolo/galase e nngwe, tsweetswee.** *keyko•pah leh•bore•tlo•loh/ga•lah•se e n•ngwe, tswe•tswe*
I'd like a local beer.	**Ke kopa biri ya selegae.** *ke ko•pah bea•ree yah se•le•gae*
Can I buy you a drink?	**A nka go rekela sengwe sa go nwa?** *ah n•kar go reh•keh•lah se•ngwe sa go n•wa*
Cheers!	**Cheers!** *cheers*
A coffee/tea, please.	**Kofi/tee, tsweetswee.** *coffea/te•eh*
Black.	**ntsho** *n•tsho*
With...	**e e nang le** *e e nang le ...*
milk	**mashi** *marsh•ee*
sugar	**sukiri** *sue•qi•re*
artificial sweetener	**sukiri ya maitirelo** *sue•qi•ree yah mar•ee•tea•reh•low*
A..., please.	**Ke kopa...., tsweetswee.** *ke ko•pah ...*
juice	**juse** *joo•ce*
soda [soft drink]	**soda [senotsididi]** *se•no•tsee•dee•dee*
(sparkling/still)	**metsi (a a nang le dipudula/a a se nang**
water	**dipudula)** *meh•tsee a a nang le dee•pu•doo•lah/a a se nang dee•pu•doo•lah*

Leisure Time

Sightseeing

Where's the tourist information office?	**Ofisi ya tshedimosetso ya bajanala e kae?** *off•ee• see yah tshe•dee•mos•air•tso yah bow•jar•nah•lah e kae*
What are the main sights?	**Mafelomagolo a ketelo ke afe?** *mar•fe•low•mar• golo a keh•teh•low key ah•fe*
Do you offer tours in English?	**A le neela maeto ka English?** *ah le neh•air•lah mar• air•tow ka English*
Can I have a map/ guide?	**Ke kopa mmapa/kaedi.** *key core•par m•mar•par/car• air•dee*

Shopping

Where's the market/ mall?	**Mmaraka/mmolo o kae?** *m•mar•rah•kar/ mall o ka•eh*
I'm just looking.	**Ke leba fela.** *ke le•bar fe•lah*
Can you help me?	**Ke kopa thuso.** *ke ko•pa o two•soh*
I'm being helped.	**Go na le yo o nthusang.** *go nah le yo oh n•two•sah•ng*
How much?	**Ke bokae?** *ke bo•kar•eh*
That one, please.	**Ke kopa ele, tsweetswee.** *ke ko•pa air•leh•tswe•tswe*
I'd like . . .	**Ke kopa . . .** *ke ko pa*
That's all.	**Ke gone gotlhe.** *ke go•neh go•tlhe*
Where can I pay?	**Ke duela kwa kae?** *ke doo•eh•lah q•waa kar•eh*

YOU MAY SEE...

BUTSWE/TSWETSWE	open/closed
MATSENO/KGORO YA GO TSWA	entrance/exit

I'll pay in cash/ by credit card.	**Ke tlaa duela ka madi a seatleng/ka karata ya sekoloto.** *ke tlaa doo·eh·lah kar mar·dee ah seh·ah·tleng/kar ckrrat·ah yah credit*
A receipt, please.	**Ke kopa rasiti, tsweetswee.** *ke ko·par rah·sea·tea*

Sport & Leisure

When's the game?	**Motshameko o leng?** *mow·tsha·meh·koh o leng*
Where's…?	**…kae?** *kar·eh*
the beach	**bitšhi (e kae?)** *beach e kar·eh*
the park	**phaka (e kae?)** *park*
the pool	**phulu (e kae?)** *pool*
Is it safe to swim here?	**A go babalesegile go thumela mo?** *ah go bar·bar·leh·seh·gile go two·meh·lah mow*
Can I hire clubs?	**A nka hira ditlelapo?** *ah n·kah hee·rah dee·club*
How much per hour/ day?	**Ke bokae ka ura/letsatsi?** *ke boh·kar·eh kar oo·rah/le·tsa·tsi*
How far is it to…?	**Go bokgakala jo bo kana kang go ya kwa …?** *go bore·kga·ka·lah jor bo kar·nah kar·ng go yah q·waa*
Show me on the map, please.	**Mpontshe mo mmapeng, tsweetswee.** *m·pon·seh mow m·mar·peng, tswe·tswe*

Going Out

What's there to do at night?	**Go na le eng se motho a ka se dirang mo bosigong jo?** *go nah le eng seh mow•tow ah kar seh dee•rang mow boo•sea•gong jor*
Do you have a program of events?	**A lo na le lenaneo la ditiragalo?** *ah low nah le leh•nah•ney•oh lah dee•tea•rah•galo*
What's playing tonight?	**Go tshameka eng bosigo jo?** *go tsha•me•ka eng bore•sea•go jor*
Where's...?	**...kae?** *...kar•eh?*
the downtown area	**lefelo la downtown (le kae)** *le•fe•low la downtown*
the bar	**bara (e kae)** *bar•ah*
the dance club	**tlelapo ya tantshe (e kae)** *tle•lah•pow yah tar•n•tshe*
Is this area safe at night?	**A lefelo le le babalesegile bosigo?** *ah le•fe•low le le bar•bar•leh•seh•gile bore•sea•go*

Baby Essentials

Do you have...?	**A o na le ...?** *ah o nah leh...*
a baby bottle	**lebotlolo la ngwana** *leh•bore•tlo•loh lah ngwa•nah*
baby food	**dijo tsa ngwana** *dee•jor tsa ngwa•nah*
baby wipes	**diphimodi tsa ngwana** *dee•pee•mudee tsa ngwa•nah*
a car seat	**setulo sa koloi** *sea•two•low sa kore•loh•ee*
a children's menu/ portion	**menyu wa bana/dijo tsa bana** *menu wah bar•nah/ dee•jor tsah bar•nah*
a child's seat/ highchair	**setulo sa ngwana/setulo se se kwa godimo** *sea•two•low sa ngwa•nah/sea•two•low se se q•waa go•dee•mow*
a crib/cot	**khoto** *core•tow*
diapers [nappies]	**metseto** *meh•tse•toh*

formula	**mashii a lebotlolo** *marsh•ee ah leh•bore•tlo•low*
a pacifier [dummy]	**tami** *taa•mee*
a playpen	**pene ya setshamekisi** *pe•neh ya se•tsha•meh•kee•sea)*
a stroller [pushchair]	**setorola (poraema)** *se•teh•row•lah/pow•rye•mar*
Can I breastfeed the baby here?	**A nka anyisetsa ngwana fa?** *ah n•kar an•yee•setsa ngwa•nah far*
Where can I breastfeed/change the baby?	**Nka anyisetsa ngwana kae/Nka fetolela kae motseto wa ngwana?** *n•kar an•yee•setsa ngwa•nah kar•eh/n•kar fe•tow•leh•lah kar•eh more•tse•to wa ngwa•nah*

For Eating Out, see page 65.

Disabled Travelers

Is there…?	**A go na le…?** *ah go nah•leh*
access for the disabled	**mafelo a digole di tsenang mo go one** *mar•fe•loh a dee•gole dee tse•nang mo go oneh*
a wheelchair ramp	**rempe ya setulo sa maotwana** *ramp yah se•two•low•sa•mao•twa•na*
a disabled-accessible toilet	**ntlwana e e ka dirisiwang ke digole** *(n•tlwa•nah e e kar dee•ree•sea•waang ke dee•gole*
I need…	**Ke tlhoka…** *(ke tlho•kar*
assistance	**thuso** *too•sore*
an elevator [a lift]	**lifiti** *lee•fee•tea*
a ground-floor room	**phaposi e e kwa tlase** *par•poo•sea e e q•waa tla•se*
Please speak louder.	**Tsweetswee buela kwa godimonyana.** *ts•we ts•we boo•er•lah q•waa go•dee•mow nya•na*

Health & Emergencies

Emergencies

Help!	**Thusa!** *too·sah*
Go away!	**Tswa fa!** *tswa·far*
Stop, thief!	**Ema, legodu!** *eh·mar, leh·go·doo*
Get a doctor!	**Bitsa ngaka!** *bee·tsa nga·kar*
Fire!	**Molelo!** *mow·leh·loh*
I'm lost.	**Ke latlhegile** *ke lah·tlhe·gile*
Can you help me?	**Ke kopa o nthuse.** *key kore·par o n·two·sir*
Call the police!	**Bitsa mapodise!** *bee·tsa mar·paw·dee·sea*
Where's the police station?	**Seteišene sa mapodisa se kae?** *station sa mar·paw·dee·sa she kae*
My child is missing.	**Ngwanake o timetse.** *ngwa·nah keh o tee·meh·tse*

For Emergency Numbers, see page 76.

YOU MAY HEAR...

Tlatsa foromo e. *tlaa·tsa four·roh·mow eh*	Fill out this form.
Id ya gago, tsweetswee. *Id yah ga·go, ts·we ts·we*	Your ID, please.
Go diragetse leng/kae? *go dee·rah·ge·tse leng/kar·eh*	When/Where did it happen?
O lebega jang? *o le·bear·ga jar·ng*	What does he/she look like?

Health

I'm sick.	**Ke a lwala.** *ke ah lwa·lah*
I need an English-speaking doctor.	**Ke tlhoka ngaka e e buang English.** *key tlho·kar nga·car e e boo·ah·ng English*
It hurts here.	**Go botlhoko fa.** *go bo·tlho·ko far)*
Where's the pharmacy?	**Khemisi e kwa kae?** *chemi·see e q·waa kar·eh*
I'm (...months) pregnant.	**Ke na le (dikgwedi tse ...) ke le moimana.** *key nah leh dee·kgwe·dee tse... ke leh more·ee·mar·nah*
I'm on...	**Ke mo...** *ke more ...*
I'm allergic to ...	**Ke alejiki mo go ...** *ke allergic mow go...*
antibiotics	**dianthibayothiki** *dee·antibiotic*
penicillin.	**phenisilini** *penicillin*

In an emergency, dial:
999 for the police
997 for an ambulance
998 for the fire brigade

acetaminophen [paracetamol]
acetaminophen

adaptor adapotara

aid worker mothusi

and le

antiseptic cream kherime ya
anthisepotheki

aspirin aspirin

baby ngwana

a backpack bekepheke

bad maswe

bag kgetsana

Band-Aid [plasters] Band-Aid
[dipolasetara]

bandages dibandeitšhe

battleground matlhabanelo

bee notshe

beige beije

bikini bikini

bird nonyane

black ntsho

bland (food) ga di monate (dijo)

blue pududu

bottle opener sebulalebotlolo

bowl sejana

boy mosimane

boyfriend lekau

bra bra

brown boraone

camera khemera

can opener sebulamoteme

cat katse

castle kasetlele

charger tšhajara

cigarettes disakerete

cold tsididi

comb (n) kama

computer khomphiutha

condoms dikhondomo

contact lens solution metsi a lense
e e tsenngwang mo matlhong

corkscrew khokosekurufu

cup kopi

dangerous kotsi

deodorant twantshamonkgo

diabetic o na le bolwetse jwa sukiri

dog ntša

doll mpopi

fly n ntsi

fork foroko

girl mosetsana

girlfriend lekgarebe

glass galase

good siame

gray kwebu

great kgolo

green tala

a hairbrush boratšhe jwa moriri

hairspray seporei sa moriri

horse pitse

hot bolelo

husband monna

ibuprofen ibuprofen

ice kgapetla (aese)

icy tsididi

injection lomao

I'd like… Ke batla…

insect repellent sekoba ditshenekegi

jeans dijini

(steak) knife thipa

lactose intolerant …sa kgone go itshokela lakethose

large kgolo

lighter laetara

lion tau

lotion [moisturizing cream] setlolo

love lerato

matches mokgwaro)

medium …gare

monkey tshwene

museum musiamo

my …me

a nail file faele ya dinala

napkin motseto (leiri)

nurse mooki

or kgotsa

orange namune

park phaka

partner molekane

pen pene

pink pinki

plate poleite

purple phepole

pyjamas dipijama

rain pula

a raincoat jase ya pula

a (disposable) razor legare

razor blades magare

red khibidu

safari safari

salty letswai

sandals dimpaatšhane

sanitary napkins [pads] diphete (dee•pad)

scissors sekere

shampoo/conditioner shampu/ khondišinara

shoes ditlhako

small nnye

snake noga

sneakers diteki

snow kapoko

soap sesepa

socks dikausu

spicy baba

spider segokgo

spoon leswana

a sweater jeresi

stamp(s) setempe (ditempe)
suitcase sutukheisi
sun letsatsi
sunglasses diporele tsa letsatsi
sunscreen sethibelatsatsi
a sweatshirt hempe
a swimsuit diaparo tsa go thuma
a T·shirt sekipa
tampons dithampone
terrible adj . . . maswe
tie tae
tissues dithishu
toilet paper pampiri ya kwa
  ntlwaneng
toothbrush borashe jwa meno
toothpaste sesepa sa meno
tough (meat) thata (nama)
toy setshamekisi
underwear seaparo sa ka fa teng
vegetarian motho yo o jang merogo
  fela
vegan motho yo o sa jeng nama
white tshweu
with le
wife mosadi
without kwa ntle ga
yellow serolwana
your . . . gago
zoo serapa sa diphologolo

Shona

Hello/Hi.	**Mhoroi/Ndeipi?** *mho•ro•yee/ndeh•yee•pi*
Goodbye.	**Bhabhai.** *bah•bah•yee*
Yes/No/Okay.	**Hongu/Kwete/Zvakanaka.** *ho•ngu/kue•teh/ zva•car•na•car*
Excuse me! (to get attention)	**Pamusoroi.** *pah•moo•so•ro•yee*
Excuse me. (to get past)	**Pamusoroi, tipindewo.** *pah•moo•so•ro•yee, tee•pee•nde•o*
I'm sorry.	**Ndine urombo.** *ndi•ne woo•ro•mbo*
I'd like…	**Ndiri kukumbirawo…** *ndi•ree coo•coo•mbi•ra•o…*
How much?	**Imarii?** *ee•mah•ree*
And/or.	**Uye/kana.** *woo•ye/car•na*
Please.	**Ndapota.** *ndah•poh•ta*
Thank you.	**Maita basa.** *mah•yee•ta ba•sa*
You're welcome.	**Muchitendei zvenyu.** *moo•chee•teh•nde•yee zve• new*
Where's…?	**Ndekupi kune…?** *ndeh•coo•pi coo•ne…*
I'm going to…	**Ndiri kuenda ku/kwa…** *ndi•ree•coo•ye•nda coo•/ kua…*
My name is…	**Ndinonzi …** *ndi•no•nzi…*
Please speak slowly.	**Ndapota taurai zvishoma nezvishoma.** *ndah•poh•ta ta•oo•ra•yee zvi•sho•ma*
Can you repeat that?	**Mungadzokorore here?** *moo•nga•dzo•ko•ro•reh heh•reh?*
I don't understand.	**Handisi kunzwisisa.** *ha•ndi•si coo•nzwi•si•sa*
Do you speak English?	**Munotaura Chirungu here?** *moo•no•ta•oo•ra chee•ru•ngu heh•reh?*

I don't speak (much) Shona.	**Handinyatsogone Shona.** *ha·ndi·nya·tso·go·ne Sho·na*
Where's the restroom [toilet]?	**Chimbuzi ndochiwana kupi?** *chee·mboo·zee ndoh·chee·wa·ne·pee*
Help!	**Ndibatsireiwo!** *ndi·ba·tsi·reh·o*

You'll find the pronunciation of the Shona letters and words written in gray after each sentence to guide you. Simply pronounce these as if they were English. As you hear the language being spoken, you will quickly become accustomed to the local pronunciation and dialect.

Numbers

0	**zero** *ze·ro*
1	**hwani** *hwa·ni*
2	**tuu** *too*
3	**thrii** *the·ree*
4	**foo** *fo·o*
5	**faifi** *far·yee·fi*
6	**sikisi** *see·kee·si*
7	**sevheni** *sir·ve·ni*
8	**eyiti** *eh·yee·ti*
9	**naini** *na·yee·ni*
10	**teni** *teh·ni*
11	**ilevheni** *ee·leh·ve·ni*
12	**twerufu** *too·wor·roo·fu*

13	**theyitini**	*thur·yee·tee·ni*
14	**footini**	*fo·o·tee·ni*
15	**fifitini**	*fi·fi·tee·ni*
16	**sikisitini**	*see·kee·si·tee·ni*
17	**sevhenitini**	*sir·ve·nee·tee·ni*
18	**eyitini**	*ur·yee·tee·ni*
19	**nainitini**	*nah·yee·nee·tee·ni*
20	**twendi**	*too·we·nti*
21	**twendi·hwani**	
	too·we·nti·hwa·ni	
30	**theti**	*thur·ti*
40	**foti**	*fo·ti*
50	**fifiti**	*fi·fi·ti*
60	**sikisiti**	*see·kee·si·ti*
70	**sevheniti**	*sir·ve·nee·ti*
80	**eyiti**	*eh·yee·tee*
90	**nainiti**	*na·yee·nee·ti*
100	**hwani handuredhi**	
	hwa·ni han·doo·reh·di	
101	**hwani handuredhi nehwani**	
	hwa·ni han·doo·reh·di ne·hwa·ni	
200	**tuu handuredhi**	*too han·doo·reh·di*
500	**faifi handuredhi**	*far·yee·fi han·doo·reh·di*
1,000	**hwani thausendi**	
	hwa·ni thah·woo·ze·nti	
10,000	**teni thausendi**	
	teh·ni thah·woo·ze·nti	
1,000,000	**miriyoni**	*mee·ree·yo·ni*

Time

What time is it?	**Inguvai?** *ee•ngu•va•yee*
It's midday.	**Iye zvino masikati.** *ee•ye•zvi•no mah•see•car•ti*
Five past three.	**Maminitsi mashanu kubva pana thrii.** *mah•mee•nee•tsi mah•shah•noo coo•bva pah•na the•ree*
A quarter to ten.	**Kota tu teni.** *koh•ta too teh•ni*
5:30 a.m./p.m.	**5:30 mangwanani/manheru.** *5:30 mah•ngua•na•nee/mah•nhe•roo*

Days

Monday	**Muvhuro** *moo•voo•ro*
Tuesday	**Chipiri** *chee•pee•ree*
Wednesday	**Chitatu** *chee•tah•too*
Thursday	**China** *chee•na*
Friday	**Chishanu** *chee•shar•noo*
Saturday	**Mugovera** *moo•go•ve•ra*
Sunday	**Svondo** *svo•ndoh*

Dates

yesterday	**nezuro** *ne•zoo•ro*
today	**nhasi** *nha•si*
tomorrow	**mangwana** *mah•ngua•nah*
day	**zuva** *zoo•va*
week	**vhiki** *vee•kee*
month	**mwedzi** *mue•dzi*
year	**gore** *go•reh*
Happy New Year!	**Makorokoto egore dzva!** *mah•koh•roh•koh•toh eh•go•reh dzva*
Happy Birthday!	**Makorokoto ebhavhudhe!** *mah•koh•roh•koh•toh eh•bah•voo•deh*

Shona is spoken primarily in Zimbabwe and southern Zambia, although you will hear it in countries neighboring Zimbabwe. It is a Bantu language spoken by over 10 million people.

Months

January	**Ndira**	ndi•rah
February	**Kukadzi**	coo•car•dzi
March	**Kurume**	coo•roo•meh
April	**Kubvumbi**	coo•bvoo•mbi
May	**Chivabvu**	chee•va•bvoo
June	**Chikumi**	chee•coo•mi
July	**Chikunguru**	chee•coo•ngu•ru
August	**Nyamavhuvhu**	nya•mah•voo•voo
September	**Gunyana**	goo•nya•na
October	**Gumiguru**	goo•mee•goo•ru
November	**Mbudzi**	mboo•dzi
December	**Zvita**	zvi•tah

Arrival & Departure

I'm on vacation [holiday]/business.	**Ndiri pazororo/pabasa.** ndi•ree• pah•zo•ro•ro/pah•ba•sa
I'm going to...	**Ndiri kuenda ku...** ndi•ree•coo•ye•nda coo...
I'm staying at	**Ndiri kugara ku...** ndi•ree•coo•ga•ra coo...
the...Hotel.	**Hotera inonzi...** ho•teh•ra ee•no•nzi...

Money

Where's...?	**Ndekupi kune...?** *ndeh•coo•pi coo•ne...*
the ATM	**mushina wekutorera mari/ATM** *moo•shee•nah weh•coo•to•rah mah•ree/ATM*
the bank	**bhengi** *beh•ngi*
the currency exchange office	**bheruu dhichaji** *beh•roo dee•char•ji*
When does the bank open/close?	**Bhengi rinovhura/rinovhara nguvai?** *be•ngi ree•no•voo•ra/ree•no•va•ra ngu•va•yee*
I'd like to change dollars/pounds sterling/euros into ...	**Ndiri kuda kuchinja madhora/mapaunzi/mayuro kuenda ku...** *ndi•ri coo•da coo•chee•nja mah•door•ra/mah•pah•woo•nzi/mah•yu•ro coo•ye•nda coo...*
I'd like to cash traveler's cheques.	**Ndiri kuda kuchinja maturavhera cheki.** *ndi•ree coo•da coo•chee•nja mah•too•ra•ve•ra che•ki*
Can I pay in cash?	**Ndinokwanisa kubhadhara iri mari here?** *ndi•no•kua•nee•sa coo•bah•dar•ra ee•ree mah•ree heh•reh?*
Can I pay by (credit) card?	**Ndinokwanisa kubhadhara nekadhi here?** *ndi•no•kua•nee•sa coo•bah•dar•ra ne•car•di heh•reh*

For Numbers, see page 82.

YOU MAY SEE...

In Zimbabwe you can pay in US dollars, South African rand, Botswana pula and even British pounds sterling.

Getting Around

How do I get to town?	**Ndingasvike sei kutaundi?** *ndi·nga·svi·ke sir·yee coo·tah·woo·ndi?*
Where's...?	**Ndekupi kune ...?** *nde·coo·pi coo·ne...?*
the airport	**Eyapoti** *eh·ya·poh·ti*
the train station	**Chiteshi chechitima** *chee·teh·shi che·chee·tee·ma*
the bus station	**Chiteshi chebhazi** *chee·teh·shi che·bah·zee*
Is it far from here?	**Kure here nepano?** *coo·reh heh·reh neh·pah·no*
Where do I buy a ticket?	**Ndinotenga kupi tiketi?** *ndi·no·te·nga coo·pi tee·ke·ti*
A one-way/return-trip ticket to...	**Ndinoda tiketi rekuenda ku...** *ndi·no·da tee·ke·ti reh·coo·ye·nda coo...*
How much?	**Imarii?** *ee·mah·ree*
Which gate/line?	**Ndoshandisa gedhi ripi?** *ndo·shah·ndi·sa ge·di ree·pi?*
Which platform?	**Ndokwirira papi?** *ndo·kwi·ree·ra pa·pi*
Where can I get a taxi?	**Ndekupi kwandingawana tekisi?** *nde·coo·pi kua·ndi·nga·wa·na teh·kee·si?*
Take me to this address.	**Ndiendesewo panzvimbo iyi.** *ndi·ye·nde·se·o pah·nzvi·mbo ee·yee*

87

To...Airport, please.	**Ku... eyapoti, ndapota.** *coo... eh·yah·poh·ti, nda·poh·ta*
I'm in a rush.	**Ndiri kumhanya.** *ndi·ree coo·mah·nya*
Can I have a map?	**Ndingawanawo mepu here?** *ndi·nga·wa·na·o meh·poo heh·reh*

Essentials

The only reliable means of getting around Zimbabwe is by car, be it a taxi or car and driver or self-drive. The road infrastructure is reasonably good, but watch out for the potholes along the way. Alternatively, there are buses: express buses are fairly reliable and run according to a set timetable (mostly to and from the bigger cities); local buses are erratic and have no fixed schedule. These over-crowded buses wait until they are full to depart and are best avoided unless they are the only means of transport available.

88

Tickets

When's...to Victoria Falls?	**Inguvai dzinosimuka ... kuenda kuVictoria Falls?** *ee·ngu·va·yee dzi·no·see·moo·ka....coo·ye·nda cooVictoria Falls?*
the (first) bus	**bhazi (rekutanga)** *bah·zee (reh·coo·tah·nga)*
the (next) flight	**ndege (inotevera)** *nde·ge (ee·no·te·ve·ra)*
the (last) train	**chitima (chekupedzisira)** *chee·tee·ma (che·coo·pe·dzi·see·ra)*
One/Two ticket(s) please.	**Ndinoda tiketi rimwechete/matiketi...** *ndi·no·da tee·ke·ti ree·mwe·che·te/mah·tee·ke·ti*
For today/tomorrow.	**Ranhasi/ramangwana** *rah·nha·si/ra·mah·ngua·na*

A ...ticket.	**Tiketi...** tee•ke•ti
one-way	**rekuenda chete** reh•coo•ye•nda che•te
return trip	**rekuenda nekudzoka** reh•coo•ye•nda ne•coo•dzo•ka
first class	**remufesiti kirasi** reh•moo•fe•si•ti kee•ra•si
I have an e-ticket.	**Ndine tiketi nechekare.**
	ndi•ne tee•ke•ti ne•che•car•reh
How long is the trip?	**Rwendo rwacho rwakareba sei?** rwe•ndo rwa•cho
	rwa•car•reh•ba sei?
Is it a direct train?	**Chitima ichi chinonanga ikoko here?** chee•tee•ma
	ee•chi chee•no•na•nga ee•ko•ko heh•reh?
Is this the bus to...?	**Ndiro bhazi rinoenda ku... here?** ndi•ro bah•zee
	ree•no•ye•nda coo... heh•reh?
Can you tell me	**Mungandiudzewo here pekuburukurira?**
when to get off?	moo•nga•ndi•oo•dze•o heh•reh peh•coo•bu•roo•kee•ra?
I'd like to...	**Ndiri kuda ku...tiketi rangu** ndi•ree coo•da coo...
my reservation.	tee•ke•ti ra•ngu
cancel	**kanzura** car•nzu•ra
change	**chinja** chee•nja
confirm	**konifema** ko•nee•fur•ma

For Time, see page 84.

Car Hire

Where's the car hire?	**Ndekupi kwandingahaya mota?** nde•coo•pi kua•
	ndi•nga•ha•ya mo•ta?
I'd like...	**Ndiri kuda...** ndi•ree coo•da...
a cheap/small car	**mota yakachipa/diki** mo•ta ya•car•chee•pa/di•ki
an automatic/	**otomatiki/manyuari** o•to•mah•tee•ki/
a manual	mah•new•wa•ree
air conditioning	**eyakondisheni** eh•yah•ko•ndi•she•ni
a car seat	**siti remwana remumotokari** see•ti reh•mua•na
	reh•moo•mo•to•car•ree

How much...?	**I marii...?** *ee·mah·ree...?*
per day/week	**pazuva/pavhiki** *pah·zoo·va/pah·vee·ki*
Are there any	**Mune madhisikaundi here?**
discounts?	*moo·ne mah·di·si·car·woo·ndi heh·reh?*

YOU MAY HEAR...

mberi kwatakananga *mbe·ree kua·ta·car·na·nga*	straight ahead
kuruboshwe *coo·roo·bo·shwe*	left
kurudyi *coo·roo·dyi*	right
patinokona *pah·tee·no·ko·na*	around the corner
pakatarisana ne... *pah·car·ta·ree·sa·na neh...*	opposite
pamashure pe... *pah·mah·shoo·reh peh...*	behind
pamberi pe... *pah·mbe·ree peh...*	next to
tapfuura *tah·pfoo·woo·ra*	after
chamhembe/maodzanyemba *cha·mhe·mbe/mah·o·dza·nye·mba*	north/south
mabvazuva/madokero *mah·bva·zoo·va/mah·do·ke·ro*	east/west
parobhoti *pah·ro·bo·ti*	at the traffic light
panosangana migwagwa *pah·no·sa·nga·na mee·gua·gua*	at the intersection

Places to Stay

Can you recommend a hotel?	**Ndingaende kuhotera ipi?** *ndi·nga·ye·nde coo·ho·te·ra ee·pi?*
I made a reservation.	**Ndakabhuka** *nda·car·boo·car*
My name is…	**Ndinonzi…** *ndi·no·nzi*
Do you have a room…?	**Pane rumu… here?** *pah·ne roo·moo… heh·reh?*
for one/two	**yemumwechete/yevaviri** *ye·moo·mwe·che·te/ ye·va·vi·ree*
with a bathroom	**ine bhathirumu** *ee·ne bah·the·roo·moo*
with air conditioning	**ine eyakondisheni** *ee·ne eh·yah·ko·ndi·share·ni*
For…	**Kwe…** *kue…*
tonight	**usiku humwechete** *oo·see·coo who·mwe·che·te*
two nights	**usiku huviri** *oo·see·coo who·vi·ree*
one week	**vhiki** *vee·ki*
How much?	**Imarii?** *ee·mah·ree*
Is there anything cheaper?	**Pane yakati chipei here?** *pah·ne ya·car·chee·pah heh·reh?*
When's checkout?	**Tinofanirwa kubuda nguvai?** *tee·no·fa·nee·rwa coo·bu·da ngu·va·yee*
Can I leave this in the safe?	**Ndinokwanisa kuisa izvi musefa here?** *ndi·no·kua·nee·sa coo·yee·sa ee·zvi moo·sir·fa heh·reh?*
Can I leave my bags?	**Ndinokwanisa kusiya mabhegi angu here?** *ndi·no·kua·nee·sa coo·see·ya mah·beh·gee ah·ngu heh·reh?*
Can I have my bill/ a receipt?	**Ndingawanawo bhiri/risiti here?** *ndi·nga·wa·na·o bee·ree/ree·see·ti heh·reh?*
I'll pay in cash/ by credit card.	**Ndichabhadhara nemari/nekadhi.** *ndi·cha·bah·dah·ra ne·mah·ree/ne·car·di*

Communications

Where's an internet cafe?	**Ndingawana kupi indaneti kefi?** ndi·nga·wa·na coo·pi ee·nda·ne·ti ke·fi?
Can I access the internet/check my email?	**Ndinokwanisa kushandisa indaneti/kucheka imeiri here?** ndi·no·kua·nee·sa coo·shah·ndi·sa ee·nda·ne·ti/coo·che·ka ee·me·yee·ri heh·reh?
How much per half hour/hour?	**Imari pachidimbu cheawa/paawa?** ee·mah·ree pah·chee·di·mboo che·ah·wa/pah·ah·wa?
How do I connect/log on?	**Ndinokwanisa kukonekita/kupinda sei?** ndi·no·kua·nee·sa coo·ko·ne·kee·ta/coo·pee·nda se·yee?
A phone card, please.	**Ndiri kudawo kadhi reeyataimu.** ndi·ree coo·da·o car·di reh·eya·tah·yee·moo
Can I have your phone number?	**Mungandipewo nhamba yenyu (yefoni) here?** moo·nga·ndi·peh·o nha·mba yeh·new (yeh·fo·ni) heh·reh?
Here's my number/email.	**Nhamba yangu/imeiri yangu ndeiyi.** nha·mba ya·ngu/ee·meh·yee·ree ya·ngu nde·yee·yee
Call me/text me.	**Ndifonerei kana kutexta.** ndi·fo·ne·reh·yee car·na coo·tek·see·ta
I'll text you.	**Ndichakutextirai.** ndi·cha·coo·tek·see·tee·ra·yee
Email me.	**Nditumirei email.** ndi·too·mee·reh·yee email
Hello. This is…	**Mhoroi. Ndini…** mo·ro·yee. ndi·nee…
Can I speak to…?	**Ndingataurewo here na…?** ndi·nga·ta·woo·reh·o heh·reh na…?
Can you repeat that?	**Mungadzokorore here?** moo·nga·dzo·ko·ro·reh heh·reh?
I'll call back later.	**Ndichafona zvakare.** ndi·cha·fo·na zva·car·reh
Bye.	**Bhabhayi.** bah·bah·yee
Where's the post office?	**Positi ofisi iri kupi?** poh·see·ti oh·fi·si ee·ree coo·pi

I'd like to send this to…	**Ndiri kuda kutumidziri ichi ku…** *ndi·ree coo·da coo·too·mee·dzi·ra ee·chi coo…*
Can I…?	**Ndinokwanisa ku…here?** *ndi·no·kua·nee·sa coo… heh·reh?*
access the internet	**shandisa indaneti** *shah·ndi·sa ee·nda·ne·ti*
check my email	**cheka imeri** *che·ka ee·me·ree*
print	**purinda** *poo·ree·nda*
plug in/charge my laptop/iPhone/ iPad/BlackBerry?	**puraga/chaja laptop/iPhone/iPad/BlackBerry** *poo·ra·ga/cha·ja laptop/iPhone/iPad/BlackBerry*
access Skype?	**Skypa** *sky·pah*
What is the WiFi password?	**Pasiwedhi yeWIFI ndeipi?** *pah·si·wor·di yeWIFI nde·yee·pi*
Is the WiFi free?	**WIFI inobhadharwa here?** *WIFI ee·no·bah·dah·rwa heh·reh?*
Do you have bluetooth?	**Mune bluetooth here?** *moo·ne blu·tooth heh·reh*
Do you have a scanner?	**Mune sikana here?** *moo·ne si·car·na heh·reh*

The Shona are farming people, also known for their excellent craftmanship, pottery and sculpture. Traditional villages are generally run by patrilinial leaders and traditionally consisted of mud and wattle huts, **rondavels** (round-shaped huts) and livestock **kraals**. Magic and witchcraft remain important methods of social control and are often used as a means to explain various occurences and disasters.

Social Media

Are you on Facebook/ Twitter?	**Muri paFesibhuku/Twita here?** *moo·ri pahFe·si·boo·coo heh·reh*
What's your username?	**Yuzanemu yenyu ndeipi?** *you·za·ne·moo ye·new ndeh·yee·pi*
I'll add you as a friend.	**Ndichaita kuti muve shamwari yangu.** *ndi·cha·yee·ta coo·ti moo·ve shah·mua·ri ya·ngu*
I'll follow you on Twitter.	**Ndichamutevera paTwita.** *ndi·cha·moo·te·ve·ra pah·Twi·tah*
Are you following...?	**Muri kutevera... here?** *moo·ree coo·teh·ve·ra... heh·reh*
I'll put the pictures on Facebook/Twitter.	**Ndichaisa mifananidzo yacho paFesibhuku/ Twita.** *ndi·cha·yee·sa mee·fa·na·nee·dzo ya·cho pah·Fe·si·boo·coo/Twi·tah*
I'll tag you in the pictures.	**Ndichakutegai pamifananidzo yacho.** *ndi·cha·coo·teh·ga·yee pah·mee·fa·na·nee·dzo ya·cho*

Conversation

Hello!/Hi!	**Mhoroi!/Ndeipi?** *mo•ro•yee?ndeh•yee•pi*
How are you?	**Makadii?** *ma•car•di•yee*
Fine, thanks.	**Zvakanaka, ndatenda.** *zva•car•na•ka, nda•teh•nda*
Excuse me!	**Pamusoroi!** *pah•m•so•ro•yee*
Do you speak English?	**Munotaura Chirungu here?** *moo•no•ta•oo•ra chee•roo•ngu heh•reh*
What's your name?	**Munonzi ani?** *moo•no•nzi ah•nee*
My name is…	**Ndinonzi…** *ndi•no•nzi…*
Nice to meet you.	**Ndafara kusangana nemi.** *nda•fa•ra coo•sa•nga•na neh•me*
Where are you from?	**Munobva kupi?** *moo•no•bva coo•pee*
I'm from the U.K./U.S.	**Ndinobva kuUK/kuAmerica.** *ndi•no•bva cooUK/cooAmerica*
What do you do for a living?	**Munoitei muupenyu?** *moo•no•yee•teh•yee moo•peh•new*
I work for…	**Ndinoshanda ku…** *ndi•no•shar•nda coo…*
I'm a student.	**Ndiri mudzidzi** *ndi•ree moo•dzi•dzi*
I'm retired.	**Ndakazorora zvekushanda.** *nda•car•zo•ro•ra zve•coo•shar•nda*

Romance

Would you like to go out for a drink/dinner?	**Ungade here kuenda kundonwa/kundodya neni?** oo•nga•deh heh•reh coo•eh•nda coo•ndo•nua/coo•ndo•dya ne•nee
What are your plans	**Unenge uchiitei manheru/mangwana?** oo•ne•nge oo•chee•yee•teh•yee mah•nhe•roo/mah•ngua•na
Can I have your (phone) number?	**Ungandipewo nhamba yako yefoni here?** oo•nga•ndi•peh•o nha•mbah ya•koh ye•fo•ni heh•reh
Can I join you?	**Ndingabatana/ndingagarisana newe here?** ndi•nga•ba•ta•na/ndi•nga•ga•ree•sa•na ne•we heh•reh
Can I buy you a drink?	**Ndingakutengera chekunwa here?** ndi•nga•coo•teh•nge•ra che•coo•nua heh•reh
I love you.	**Ndinokuda.** ndi•no•coo•da

Accepting & Rejecting

I'd love to.	**Ndingade.** ndi•nga•de
Where should we meet?	**Tingasangane kupi?** tee•sa•nga•neh coo•pee
I'll meet you at the bar/your hotel.	**Tosangana kubhawa/kuhotera kwako.** toh•sa•nga na coo•bah•wa/coo•ho•teh•ra kua•koh
I'll come by at…	**Ndichauya nenguva dza…** ndi•cha•oo•ya neh•ngu•va dza…
I'm busy.	**Ndakabatikana.** nda•car•ba•tee•car•na
I'm not interested.	**Handidi.** ha•ndi•di
Leave me alone.	**Siyana neni.** see•ya•na neh•ni
Stop bothering me!	**Chimbomira kundinetsa!** chee•mbo•mee•ra coo•ndi•neh•tsa

Food & Drink

Eating Out

Can you recommend a good restaurant/bar?	**Ndingaende kuresitorendi ipi/bhawa ripi?** *ndi·nga·endeh coo·reh·see·toh·reh·ndi/bah·wa ree·pi*
Is there a traditional/an inexpensive restaurant nearby?	**Pane resitorendi iri pedyo inotengesa zvechinyakare/yakachipa here?** *pah·neh· reh·si·toh·reh·ndi ee·ree peh·dyo ee·no·teh·nge·sa zve·chee·nya·car·reh/ya·car·chee·pah heh·reh*
A table for..., please.	**Tinodawo tebhuru yevanhu...** *tee·no·da·o teh·boo·roo ye·va·nhu...*
Can we sit...?	**Tinokwanisa kugara...here?** *tee·no·kua·nee·sa coo·ga·ra... heh·reh*
here/there	**pano/apo** *pah·no/ah·poh*
outside	**panze** *pah·nze*
in a non-smoking area	**pasingaputwe fodya** *pah·see·nga·poo·twe fo·dya*
I'm waiting for someone.	**Ndakamirira mumwe munhu** *nda·car·mee·ree·ra moo·mwe moo·nhu*
Where are the toilets?	**Ndekupi kune chimbuzi?** *nde·coo·pi coo·neh chee·mboo·zee*
The menu, please.	**Ndipeiwo menyu.** *ndi·peh·yee·o meh·new*
What do you recommend?	**Chii chaungandikurudzire?** *chee·ee cha·oo·nga·ndi·coo·roo·dzi·reh*
I'd like...	**Ndiri kuda...** *ndi·ree coo·da*
Some more..., please.	**Ndiwedzereiwo...** *ndi·we·dze·reh·yee·o*
Enjoy your meal!	**Sunungukai zvenyu kudya chikafu chenyu!** *soo·noo·ngu·car·yee zve·new coo·dya chee·car·fu che·new*
The check [bill], please.	**Ndipeiwo bhiri.** *ndi·peh·yee·o bee·ree*

Is service included? **Maisa netipi here?** mah·yee·sa neh·tee·pi heh·reh

Can I pay by credit **Ndingabhadhare nekadhi/**
card/have a receipt? **ndingawane risiti here?** ndi·nga·bah·dah·reh neh·
car·di/ndi·nga·wa·neh ree·see·ti heh·reh

YOU MAY SEE...

KAVHACHAJI	cover charge
MUTENGO USINGACHINJI	fixed price
MENYU (YEZUVA IRORO)	menu (of the day)
TIPI YAISWA/HAINA KUISWA	service (not) included
ZVIRI PASIPESHARO	specials

Breakfast

oatmeal [porridge]	**bota** boh·tah
bread	**chingwa** chee·ngua
butter	**bhata** bah·tah
cold cuts	**nyama dzisina kudziiswa** nya·ma dzi·see·na coo·dzi·yee·swa
cheese	**chizi** chee·zee
...egg	**zai** za·yee
hard/soft boiled	**rakanyatsoibva/risina kunyanyisa kuibva** ra·car· nya·tso·yee·bva/ree·see·na ku·nya·nyi·sa coo·yee·bva
fried	**rakafuraiwa** ra·car·fu·ra·yee·wa

As in other African countries, mealie meal or cornmeal is often eaten as **bota** (porridge) in the mornings and again prepared in a different way as **sadza** for the evening meal.

scrambled	**rakaskiremburiwa** ra·car·seek·reh·mboo·ree·wa
jam/jelly	**jamu/jeli** jah·moo/je·lee
omelette	**omureti** oh·moo·reh·ti
toast	**tositi** toh·si·ti
sausage	**sochisi** so·chee·si
yogurt	**yogati** yoh·ga·ti

Appetizers

Fish soup	**Muto wehove** moo·toh weh·ho·veh
Vegetable/tomato soup	**Muto wemavheji/wemadomasi** moo·toh weh·mah·ve·ji/weh·mah·do·mah·si
Chicken soup	**Muto wehuku** moo·toh weh·hoo·coo
Salad	**Saradhi** sah·rah·di

Meat

Beef	**nyama yemombe** nya·mah ye·moh·mbe
Chicken	**huku** hoo·coo
Lamb	**nyama yehwai** nya·mah ye·hwa·yee
Pork	**nyama yenguruve** nya·mah ye·ngu·roo·veh
Steak	**mushuna** moo·shoo·nah
Veal	**nyama yakapfava** nya·mah ya·car·pfa·va

YOU MAY HEAR...

risina/isina kunyanyoibva ree·see·na/ee·see·nah coo·nya·nyo·yee·bva	rare
rakaibva/yakaibva zviri pakati nepakati rah·car·yee·bva/ya·car·yee·bva zvi·ree pah·car·tee ne·pah·car·tee	medium
rakanyatsoibva rah·car·nya·tso·yee·bva	well-done

Fish & Seafood

Cod	**kodhi**	ko·di
Fishcakes	**mafishikeke**	mah·fi·shi·keh·keh
Herring	**heringi**	heh·ree·ngi
Lobster	**gakanje**	ga·car·nje
Salmon	**Salmoni**	sahl·mo·nee
Shrimp [prawns]	**mapuronzi**	mah·poo·ro·nzi

Vegetables

Beans	**bhinzi**	bee·nzi
Cabbage	**kebheji**	keh·beh·ji
Carrots	**makerotsi**	keh·ro·tsi
Mushroom	**hohwa**	ho·wa
Onion	**hanyanisi**	hah·nya·nee·si
Peas	**pizi**	pee·zee
Potato	**mbatatisi**	mba·tah·tee·si
Tomato	**domasi**	do·mah·si

Sauces & Condiments

Salt	**sauti**	sah·oot
Pepper	**mhiripiri**	mhi·ree·pee·ree
Mustard	**masitadhi**	mass·tar·di
Ketchup	**tomatososi**	toh·mah·toh·so·si

Fruit & Dessert

apple	**apuro**	ah·poo·roh
banana	**bhanana**	bah·nah·nah
lemon	**remani**	reh·mah·ni
orange	**ranjisi**	rah·nji·si
pear	**peya**	peh·yah
strawberries	**siturobheri**	see·too·roh·beh·ree
ice cream	**aizikirimu**	a·yee·zee·kee·ree·moo

chocolate/vanilla	**chokoreti/vanilla** cho•ko•reh•ti/va•nee•lah
tart/cake	**keke** ke•ke
mousse	**musi** moo•si
custard/cream	**kasitadhi/kirimu** car•si•tar•di/kee•ree•moo

Drinks

The wine list/drink menu, please.	**Ndipeiwo menyu yemawaini/zvinwiwa.** ndi•peh•yee•o meh•new ye•mah•wa•yee•nee/zvi•nwi•wa
What do you recommend?	**Chii chaungandikurudzire?** chee•yee cha•oo•nga•ndi•coo•roo•dzi•reh
I'd like a bottle/glass of red/white wine.	**Ndiri kuda bhodhoro/girazi reredhi/waiti waini.** ndi•ree coo•da boh•doh•roh/gee•rah•zee reh•reh•di/wa•yee•ti wa•yee•ni
The house wine, please.	**Ndipeiwo hausi waini.** ndi•peh•yee•o hah•oo•si wa•yee•ni
Another bottle/glass, please.	**Ndipeiwo rimwe bhodhoro/girazi.** ndi•peh•yee•o ree•mwe boh•doh•roh/gee•rah•zee
I'd like a local beer.	**Ndiri kuda doro remuno.** ndi•ri coo•da do•roh reh•moo•no
Can I buy you a drink?	**Ndingakutengera chekunwa here?** ndi•nga•coo•teh•nge•rah che•coo•nwa heh•reh

Cheers!	**Chiyezi!** *chee·ye·zee*
A coffee/tea, please.	**Ndipeiwo kofi/tii.** *ndi·peh·o ko·fee/tee*
Black.	**Tii isina mukaka** *tee ee·see·na moo·car·car*
With…	**Ine…** *ee·neh*
milk	**mukaka** *moo·car·car*
sugar	**shuga** *shoo·ga*
artificial sweetener	**zvekuti itapire** *zve·coo·ti ee·tah·pee·reh*
A…, please.	**Ndipeiwo** *ndi·peh·yee·o*
juice	**jusi** *joo·si*
soda [soft drink]	**sofuti dhuringi** *so·foo·ti doo·ree·ngi*
(sparkling/still) water	**mvura** *mvoo·rah*

Leisure Time

Sightseeing

Where's the tourist information office?	**Ndekupi kune hofisi yekupa vashanyi ruzivo?** *nde·coo·pi coo·neh ho·fi·si ye·coo·pah va·shar·nyi roo·zee·vo*
What are the main sights?	**Ndezvipi zvinonyanyoonekwa?** *nde·zvi·pi zvi·no·nya·nyo·o·neh·kua*
Do you offer tours in English?	**Munotenderedza vashanyi muchitaura neChiringu here?** *moo·no·teh·nde·reh·dza va·shar·nyi moo·chee·ta·oo·ra ne·chee·roo·ngu heh·reh*

YOU MAY SEE…

| PAKAVHURWA/PAKAVHARWA | open/closed |
| KUPINDA/KUBUDA | entrance/exit |

| Can I have a map/ guide? | **Ndingawanawo mepu/gaidhi here?** *ndi·nga·wa· na·o meh·poo/ga·yee·di heh·reh* |

Shopping

Where's the market/ mall?	**Musika uripi/mall iripi?** *moo·see·car oo·ree·pi/mol ee·ree·pi*
I'm just looking.	**Ndiri kungoona zvangu.** *ndi·ree coo·ngo·o·na zva· ngu*
Can you help me?	**Mungandibatsirawo here?** *moo·nga·ndi·ba·tsi· reh·o heh·reh*
I'm being helped.	**Pane ari kundibatsira.** *pah·neh ah·ree coo·ndi·ba· tsi·rah*
How much?	**Imarii?** *ee·mah·ree*
That one, please.	**Icho, ndapota** *ee·cho, nda·poh·ta*
I'd like…	**Ndiri kuda…** *ndi·ree coo·da…*
That's all.	**Ndizvo chete.** *ndi·zvo cheh·teh*
Where can I pay?	**Ndobhadhara kupi?** *ndo·bah·dah·rah coo·pi*
I'll pay in cash/ by credit card.	**Ndichabhadhara nemari/nekadhi.** *ndi·cha·bah· dah·rah neh·mah·ree/neh·car·di*
A receipt, please.	**Ndipeiwo risiti.** *ndi·peh·yee·o ree·see·ti*

Sport & Leisure

When's the game?	**Riri kutambwa rinhi?** *ree·ri coo·ta·mbwa ree·ni*
Where's...?	**Ndekupi kune...?** *nde·coo·pi coo·neh...*
the beach	**bhichi** *bee·chi*
the park	**paki** *pah·ki*
the pool	**puru** *poo·roo*
Is it safe to swim here?	**Hazvina njodzi here kutuhwina umu?** *ha·zvi·na njo·dzi heh·reh coo·too·hwi·na oo·moo*
Can I hire clubs?	**Ndinokwanisa kuhaya makirabhu here?** *ndi·no·kua·nee·sa coo·ha·ya mah·kee·rah·buh heh·reh*
How much per hour/day?	**Imarii paawa/pazuva?** *ee·mah·ree pah·ah·wa/pah·zoo·va*
How far is it to...?	**Pano ne...pakareba sei?** *pah·no neh... pah·car·reh·ba sir·ee*
Show me on the map, please.	**Ndiratidzeiwo pamepu.** *ndi·ra·tee·dze·ee·o pah·meh·poo*

Going Out

What's there to do at night?	**Chii chandingaite manheru?** *chee·ee cha·ndi·nga·yee·teh mah·nhe·roo*
Do you have a program of events?	**Mune purogiramu yezvinenge zvichiitika here?** *moo·neh poo·ro·gee·ra·moo ye·zvi·neh·nge zvi·chee·yee·tee·car heh·reh*
What's playing tonight?	**Ndiani ari kuridza nhasi manheru?** *ndi·ya·nee ah·ree coo·ree·dza nha·si mah·nhe·roo*
Where's...?	**Ndekupi kune ...?** *nde·coo·pi coo·neh...*
the downtown area	**kudhaunitauni** *coo·dah·woo·nee·ta·woo·nee*
the bar	**bhawa** *bah·wah*
the dance club	**dhanzi kirabhu** *dah·nzi kee·ra·boo*
Is this area safe at night?	**Nzvimbo ino haina njodzi here kana ave manheru?** *nzvi·mbo ee·no ha·yee·na njo·dzi heh·reh car·na ah·veh mah·nhe·roo*

Baby Essentials

Do you have...?	**Mungaitewo ...here?** *moo·nga·yee·teh·o... heh·reh*
a baby bottle	**bhodhoro remwana** *boh·doh·ro reh·mua·na*
baby food	**chikafu chemwana** *chee·car·fu che·mua·na*
baby wipes	**zvekupukutisa mwana** *zve·coo·poo·coo·tee·sa mua·na*
a car seat	**siti remwana remumotokari** *see·ti reh·mua·na reh·moo·mo·tah*
a children's menu/ portion	**menyu yevana** *meh·new ye·va·na*
a child's seat/ highchair	**cheya yevana** *che·ya ye·mua·na*
a crib/cot	**pekurarisa vana** *peh·coo·rah·ree·sa va·na*
diapers [nappies]	**maphamba** *mah·pah·mba*

formula	**mukaka wevana** *moo·car·car weh·va·na*
a pacifier [dummy]	**chekuvaraidza mwana** *che·coo·va·ra·yee·dza mua·na*
a playpen	**panotambira vacheche** *pah·no·tah·mbi·rah va·cheh·cheh*
a stroller [pushchair]	**purema** *poo·reh·ma*
Can I breastfeed the baby here?	**Ndingayamwisa mwana pano here?** *ndi·nga·ya·mwi·sa mua·na pah·no heh·reh*
Where can I breastfeed/change the baby?	**Ndingayamwisira/ndingachinjira mwana kupi?** *ndi·nga·ya·mwi·see·rah/ndi·nga·chee·nji·rah mua·na coo·pi?*

For Eating Out, see page 97.

Disabled Travelers

Is there…?	**Pane here…?** *pah·neh heh·reh*
access for the disabled	**panoendwa napo nevakaremara** *pah·no·eh·ndwa na·poh neh·va·car·reh·mah·rah*
a wheelchair ramp	**panofamba wiricheya** *pah·no·fa·mba wee·ree·che·ya*
a disabled-accessible toilet	**chimbuzi chevakaremara** *chee·mbu·zee che·va·car·reh·mah·rah*
I need…	**Ndinoda…** *ndi·no·da*
assistance	**rubatsiro** *roo·ba·tsi·ro*
an elevator [a lift]	**rifiti** *ree·fi·ti*
a ground-floor room	**rumu yepasi** *roo·moo ye·pah·si*
Please speak louder.	**Ndapota taurai muchisheedzera.** *nda·poh·tah tah·oo·rah·yee moo·chee·sheh·veh·dze·ra*

106

Health & Emergencies

Emergencies

Help!	**Ndibatsireiwo!** *ndi·ba·tsi·reh·yee·o*
Go away!	**Ibva pano!** *ee·bva pah·no*
Stop, thief!	**Batai, mbavha!** *ba·tah·yee mba·va*
Get a doctor!	**Ndiendesei kuna chiremba!** *ndi·eh·nde·seh·yee coo·na chee·reh·mba*
Fire!	**Moto!** *moh·to*
I'm lost.	**Ndarasika.** *nda·rah·see·ka*
Can you help me?	**Mungandibatsirawo here?** *moo·nga·ndi·ba·tsi·rah·o heh·reh*
Call the police!	**Sheedzai mapurisa!** *sheh·eh·dza·yee mah·poo·ree·sa*
Where's the police station?	**Kamba yemapurisa iri kupi?** *car·mba ye·mah·poo·ree·sa ee·ree coo·pi*
My child is missing.	**Mwana wangu arasika.** *mua·na wa·ngu ah·rah·see·ka*

YOU MAY HEAR...

Zadzisai fomu iri. *za·dzi·sa fo·moo ee·ree*	Fill out this form.
Ndipeiwo chitupa chenyu/ID yenyu. *ndi·peh·yee·o chee·too·pah che·new/ID ye·new*	Your ID, please.
Irinhi/ndekupi kwazvakaitika. *ee·ree·nhi/nde·coo·pi kua·zva·car·yee·tee·car*	When/Where did it happen?
Akaita sei munhu wacho? *ah·car·yee·ta sir·yee moo·nhu wa·cho*	What does he/she look like?

In Harare, dial **999** in the case of an emergency. From a cell phone you can dial **112**.
In any other areas, please check numbers locally upon arrival.

Health

I'm sick.	**Ndiri kurwara.** *ndi·ree coo·rwa·rah*
I need an English-speaking doctor.	**Ndiri kuda chiremba anotaura Chirungu.** *ndi·ree coo·da chee·reh·mba ah·no·tah·oo·rah chee·roo·ngu*
It hurts here.	**Ndiri kurwadziwa nepapa.** *ndi·ree coo·rwa·dzi·wa neh·pah·pah*
Where's the pharmacy?	**Ndekupi kune famasi?** *nde·coo·pi coo·neh fa·mah·see*
I'm (...months) pregnant.	**Pamuviri pangu pane mwedzi...** *pah·moo·vi·ree pah·ngu pah·neh mue·dzi...*
I'm on...	**Ndiri kutora...** *ndi·ree coo·to·rah...*
I'm allergic to antibiotics/penicillin.	**Muviri wangu hauwirirane ne·maantibhayotiki/ penisirini.** *moo·vi·ree wa·ngu how·wi·ree·rah·neh neh mah·ah·ndi·bah·yo·tiks/peh·nee·see·ree·ni*

a aa

acetaminophen [paracetamol] parasetamoro

adaptor adhaputa

aid worker mushandi anobatsira vanhu

and uye

antiseptic cream kirimu inouraya majemusi

aspirin asipurini

baby mwana

a backpack bhegi rekubereka

bad zvakaipa

bag bhegi

Band-Aid [plasters] kabhandeji

bandages bhandeji

battleground panorwirwa

bee nyuchi

beige pfumbu

bikini bhikini

birds shiri

black nhema

bland (food) blandi (chikafu)

blue bhuruu

bottle opener opena yemabhodhoro

bowl bhawero

boy mukomana

boyfriend mudiwa wechirume

bra bhurezha

brown bhurauni

camera kamera

can opener opena yemagaba

cat katsi

castle muzinda

charger chaja

cigarettes midzanga

cold chando/kutonhora

comb (n) kamu

computer kombiyuta

condoms makondomu

contact lens solution mushonga wekuisa pamagirazi ekumeso

corkscrew chekuvhurisa bhodhoro rewaini

cup kapu

dangerous zvine njodzi

deodorant pefiyumu

diabetic ane shuga

dog imbwa

doll chidhori

fly (noun) nhunzi

fork forogo

girl musikana

girlfriend mudiwa wechikadzi

glass girazi

good zvakanaka

gray pfumbu

great chihombe
green girinhi
a hairbrush bhurashi remusoro
hairspray zvekupfapfaidza musoro
horse bhiza
hot kupisa
husband murume
ibuprofen mabhurufeni
ice chando
icy zvine chando
injection jekiseni
I'd like... Ndiri kuda...
insect repellent mushonga
   unodzinga tubhururukwa
jeans majini
(steak) knife banga rekudyisa
   nyama
lactose intolerant kufufutirwa
large chihombe
lighter chakareruka
lion shumba
lotion [moisturizing cream]
   losheni
love rudo
matches machisi
medium pakati nepakati
monkey tsoko
museum miziyamu
my changu
a nail file chekurodzesa nzara
napkin napukeni

nurse nesi
or kana
orange ranjisi
park phaka
partner mumwe wangu
pen chinyoreso
pink pingi
plate ndiro
purple pepuru
pyjamas mapijama
rain mvura inonaya
a raincoat renikoti
razor reza
razor blades mareza
red chitsvuku
safari safari
salty chine munyu
sandals masandurosi
sanitary napkins [pads] mapedzi
scissors chigero
shampoo/conditioner sipo
   yekugezesa musoro
shoes shangu
small chidiki
snake nyoka
sneakers mateki
snow chando
soap sipo
socks masokisi
spicy zvinovavira
spider sipaidha

110

spoon chipunu
a sweater siweta
stamp(s) zvitambi
suitcase sutukezi
sun zuva
sunglasses magirazi ezuva
sunscreen mafuta ekuderedza
  kutsva nezuva
a sweatshirt juzi
a swimsuit chipfeko
  chekutuhwinisa
a T·shirt tiisheti
tampons matambuni
terrible zvakaipisisa
tie tayi
tissues matishu
toilet paper matishu emutoireti
toothbrush tuthubhurashi
toothpaste mushonga wemazino
tough (meat) kuomarara
  (nyama)
toy toyi
underwear zvipfeko zvemukati
vegetarian asingadyi nyama
vegan asingadyi kana kushandisa
  chose zvacho pamhuka
white chichena
with na/ne-
wife mukadzi
without pasina
yellow yero

your chako
zoo panogara mhuka

Afrikaans

Essentials

Hello/Hi.	**Hallo/Hey.** *Hell·oh/Hay.*
Goodbye.	**Totsiens.** *Taut·seens.*
Yes/No/Okay.	**Ja/Nee/Okay.** *Ya/Ni·yee/Oh·kay*
Excuse me!	**Ekskuus tog!** *Ehk·ski's toch!*
(to get attention)	
Excuse me.	**Verskoon my.** *Fir·skoon may!*
(to get past)	
I'm sorry.	**Ek's jammer** *Axe yam·mirr*
I'd like…	**Ek soek….** *Ack sook…*
How much?	**Hoeveel?** *Who·feel?*
And/or.	**En/of.** *Ehn/awf.*
Please.	**Asseblief.** *Us·sih·bleaf*
Thank you.	**Dankie.** *Dung·key.*
You're welcome.	**Jy's welkom.** *Yay's vell·com.*
Where's…?	**Waar's…?** *Vaahr's…?*
I'm going to…	**Ek gaan na…** *Ack chaan naah…*
My name is…	**My naam is…** *May nahm is…*
Please speak slowly.	**Praat asseblief stadig.** *Praht us·sih·bleaf stah·dich.*
Can you repeat that?	**Kan jy dit herhaal?** *Cunn yay dit herr·haal?*
I don't understand.	**Ek verstaan nie.** *Ack fir·stahn knee.*
Do you speak English?	**Praat jy Engels?** *Praaht yay Aeng·ils?*
I don't speak (much) Afrikaans.	**Ek praat nie baie Afrikaans nie.** *Ack praht knee buy·a Af·ree·kaans knee.*
Where's the restroom [toilet]?	**Waar is die kleedkamer?** *Vaahr is dee kliyeed·kahmir?*
Help!	**Help!** *Help!*

You'll find the pronunciation of the Afrikaans letters and words written in gray after each sentence to guide you. Simply pronounce these as if they were English. As you hear the language being spoken, you will quickly become accustomed to the local pronunciation and dialect.

Numbers

0	**nul**	*nil*
1	**een**	*ian*
2	**twee**	*too·wiye*
3	**drie**	*dree*
4	**vier**	*fiir*
5	**vyf**	*fayf*
6	**ses**	*ses*
7	**sewe**	*si·ye·ve*
8	**agt**	*acht*
9	**nege**	*ne·che*
10	**tien**	*teen*
11	**elf**	*elf*
12	**twaalf**	*too·aalf*
13	**dertien**	*dehr·teen*
14	**veertien**	*fear·teen*
15	**vyftien**	*fayf·teen*
16	**sestien**	*ses·teen*
17	**sewentien**	*siye·vin·teen*
18	**agtien**	*ach·teen*
19	**negentien**	*knee·a·chin·teen*
20	**twintig**	*twin·tich*

Please note: '**ch**' represents a guttural sound, like clearing your throat while exhaling, i.e. with the back of the tongue close to or touching the soft palate. Make a '**h**' sound, remembering to let the air flow freely. While you are making this sound, reduce the gap between the roof of your mouth and the back of your tongue until friction becomes audible.

It is not the same as the '**ch**' in Jackie Chan, China, or cheque, which is a palato-alveolar affricate sound, but rather like the Scots talking about the Lo**ch** Ness monster.

'**ng**' represents a nasal sound at the back of your throat, also while exhaling. It is a velar nasal sound, like the English word, 'si**ng**'.

21	**een·en·twintig**	ian·ehn·twin·tich
30	**dertig**	daer·tich
40	**veertig**	fear·tich
50	**vyftig**	fyf·tich
60	**sestig**	ses·tich
70	**sewentig**	siye·vin·tich
80	**tagtig**	tach·tich
90	**negentig**	niye·chin·tich
100	**een honderd**	ian·hawn·dird
101	**honderd·en·een**	hawn·dird·(h)en·ian
200	**twee honderd**	two·wiye·hawn·dird
500	**vyf honderd**	fyf hawn·dird
1,000	**een duisend**	ian·duay·sind
10,000	**tien duisend**	teen·duay·sind
1,000,000	**'n miljoen**	ih mill·yune

Time

What time is it?	**Hoe laat is dit?** *Who laat ihs diht?*
It's midday.	**Dis middag.** *Dis mid·dach.*
Five past three.	**Vyf oor drie.** *Fyf oohr dree*
A quarter to ten.	**Kwart voor tien.** *Quwart foor teen*
5:30 a.m./p.m.	**5:30 v.m/n.m** *fyf dehrtich fee em/en em*

Days

Monday	**Maandag** *Maan·dach*
Tuesday	**Dinsdag** *Dins·dach*
Wednesday	**Woensdag** *Voons·dach*
Thursday	**Donderdag** *Dawn·dir·dach*
Friday	**Vrydag** *Fray·dach*
Saturday	**Saterdag** *Sa·tir·dach*
Sunday	**Sondag** *Sawn·dach*

Dates

yesterday	**gister** *chis·tir*
today	**vandag** *fun·dach*
tomorrow	**môre** *more·ih*
day	**dag** *dach*
week	**week** *vi·ye·k*
month	**maand** *maahnd*
year	**jaar** *yaar*
Happy New Year!	**Gelukkige Nuwe Jaar!** *Chi·luhk·ihche Nu·ve Yaar!*
Happy Birthday!	**Geluk met jou verjaardag!** *Chi·luhk met yi·oh fir·yaar·dach!*

Months

January	**Januarie** *Yanu·aree*
February	**Februarie** *Febru·ahree*
March	**Maart** *Maart*
April	**April** *Ah·pril*
May	**Mei** *May*
June	**Junie** *Juh·knee*
July	**Julie** *Juh·lee*
August	**Augustus** *Au·chus·tus*
September	**September** *Sip·tem·bir*
October	**Oktober** *Ock·too·bir*
November	**November** *No·vem·ber*
December	**Desember** *De·sem·bir*

Afrikaans is spoken in South Africa and parts of Namibia by approximately 7 million people.

Arrival & Departure

I'm on vacation [holiday]/business.	**Ek's op vakansie/besigheid.** *Axe awp fa•cunn•see/biye•sich•hate.*
I'm going to…	**Ek is op pad na…** *Ack is awp put naah…*
I'm staying at the…Hotel.	**Ek bly by die ….Hotel.** *Ack blay bay dee…who•tell.*

Money

Where's…?	**Waar's…?** *Vaahr's…?*
the ATM	**die OTM** *dee Oh•Tee•Em*
the bank	**die bank** *dee bahngk*
the currency exchange office	**die geldwissel kantoor** *dee cheld•vis•sill cunn•toohr*
When does the bank open/close?	**Wanneer maak die bank oop/toe?** *Vahn•near mahk die bank oop/touh?*
I'd like to change dollars/pounds sterling/euros into Rand.	**Ek wil graag dollers/ponde/euro na Rand omruil.** *Ack vil chraach doll•lihrs/pawn•de/ ye•ro nah rahnd awm•ray•il.*

YOU MAY SEE...

The currency in South Africa is the **South African Rand**. R1 = 100 cent.
Coins: R1, R2, R5, 5c, 10c, 20c
Notes: R10, R20, R50, R100, R200

I'd like to cash traveler's cheques.	**Ek wil graag die reisigerstjeks omruil in kontant.** *Ack vil chraach dee rayse•chirs•cheques awm•ruayl ihn kawn•tunt.*
Can I pay in cash?	**Kan ek met kontant betaal?** *Cunn ack met kawn•tunt be•taal?*
Can I pay by (credit) card?	**Kan ek met die kaart betaal?** *Cunn ack met dee kaart bih•taahl?*

For Numbers, see page 114.

Getting Around

How do I get to town?	**Hoe kom ek by die dorp uit?** *Who kawm ack bay dee dawrp uayt?*
Where's...?	**Waar's...?** *Vaahrs...?*
the airport	**die lughawe** *dee luch•hah•vih*
the train station	**die treinstasie** *dee train•stah•see*
the bus station	**die busstasie** *dee buhs•sta•see*

Incidents involving tourists in South Africa are comparatively
rare but take the usual precautions you would in any big city. If
you need to stop to consult a map or guide, walk into a shop or bank
rather than standing looking lost on a street corner.

Is it far from here?	**Is dit ver van hier af?**	
	Is dit fehr fan hiir af?	
Where do I buy a ticket?	**Waar koop ek 'n kaartjie?**	
	Vaahr kou•whip ack i kaar•key?	
A one-way/return-trip ticket to...	**'n Eenrigting/retoerkaartjie na...**	
	ih ian•rich•ting/ri•tuur•kaar•key nah...	
How much?	**Hoeveel?** *Who•feel?*	
Which gate/line?	**Watter hek/lyn?**	
	Vaht•tir hack/lain?	
Which platform?	**Watter platform?**	
	Vaht•tir plutt•faw•rim?	
Where can I get a taxi?	**Waar kan ek 'n huurmotor kry?**	
	Vaahr cunn ack ih huur•mo•tor kray?	
Take me to this address.	**Neem my na hierdie adres.** *Ni•yeem may nah hiir•dee ah•dres.*	
To...Airport, please.	**Na...Lughawe, asseblief.**	
	Nah...Luch•hah•vih, us•sih bleaf.	
I'm in a rush.	**Ek is haastig.** *Ack ihs haas•tich.*	
Can I have a map?	**Kan ek 'n kaart kry?**	
	Cunn ack ih kaart kry?	

Tickets

When's...to Durban?	**Wanneer is ...na Durban?**	
	Vahn•near is...nah Durban?	
the (first) bus	**die (eerste) bus** *dee (ear•stih)bus*	
the (next) flight	**die (volgende) vlug** *dee (fawl•chin•dih) vlug*	
the (last) train	**die (laaste) trein** *dee (laas•tih) train*	
One/Two ticket(s) please.	**Een/Twee kaartjie(s) asseblief.** *Ian/Too•wiye kaar•key(s) us•sih•bleaf*	
For today/tomorrow.	**Vir vandag/môre.**	
	Fir fun•dach/more•ih	

A…ticket.	**'n Kaartjie.** *ih…caar•key*	
one-way	**eenrigting** *ian•rich•ting*	
return trip	**retoer** *rih•toohr*	
first class	**eerste klas** *ear•stih•klus*	
I have an e-ticket.	**Ek het 'n e•kaartjie.** *Ack het ih ee•caar•key.*	
How long is the trip?	**Hoe lank is die reis?** *Who lungk is dee race?*	
Is it a direct train?	**Is dit 'n direkte trein?** *Is dit ih dee•rec•tih train?*	
Is this the bus to…?	**Is hierdie die bus na…?** *Is heer•dee dee buhs nah…?*	
Can you tell me when to get off?	**Kan jy vir my sê wanneer om af te klim?** *Cunn yay fir may seh van•ny•eer awm ahf tih klihm?*	121
I'd like to… my reservation.	**Ek wil graag my bespreking…** *Ack vihl chraach may bih•spreh•king…*	
cancel	**kanselleer** *cunn•sih•liyeer*	
change	**verander** *fir•ahn•dir*	
confirm	**bevestig** *bih•fes•tich*	

For Time, see page 116.

Car Hire

Where's the car hire?	**Waar is die motorhuur?**	*Vaahr ihs dee muotir•huur?*
I'd like…	**Ek soek 'n…**	*Ack sook ih…*
a cheap/small car	**'n goedkoop/klein kar**	*ih chude•kuwip/klain kar*
an automatic/ a manual	**'n outomatiese/handstuur**	*ih au•toh•mah•tee•sih/ hunt•stuhr*
air conditioning	**lugversorging**	*luch•fir•sawhr•ching*
a car seat	**'n karstoel**	*ih kar•stool*
How much…?	**Hoe baie…?**	*Who bye•ih…?*
per day/week	**per dag/week**	*per dach/viy•eek*
Are there any discounts?	**Is daar enige afslag?**	*Is dahr ee•niche af•slach?*

YOU MAY HEAR…

reguit vorentoe *rech•uyt fo•rin•two*	straight ahead
links *lingks*	left
regs *rechs*	right
om die hoek *awm dee hook*	around the corner
oorkant *oohr•kant*	opposite
agter *ach•tihr*	behind
langs *langs*	next to
na *naah*	after
noord/suid *noo•wird/suyt*	north/south
oos/wes *oo•is/vess*	east/west
by die verkeerslig *bay dee fir•keers•lich*	at the traffic light
by die kruising *bay dee kray•sing*	at the intersection

Places to Stay

Can you recommend a hotel?	**Kan jy 'n hotel aanbeveel?** *Cunn yay ih who·tel aan·be·veel?*
I made a reservation.	**Ek het 'n bespreking gemaak.** *Ack het ih bih·spre·king che·maahk.*
My name is…	**My naam is…** *May naam is….*
Do you have a room…?	**Het jy 'n kamer…?** *Het yay ih kah·mer…?*
for one/two	**vir een/twee** *fir ian/too·wiye*
with a bathroom	**met 'n badkamer** *met ih baht·kah·mir*
with air conditioning	**met lugversorging** *met luch·fir·sohr·ching*
For…	**Vir…** *fir…*
tonight	**vanaand** *fi·naahnd*
two nights	**twee nagte** *too·wiye nach·tih*
one week	**een week** *ian vyeek*
How much?	**Hoeveel?** *Who·fiyeel?*
Is there anything cheaper?	**Is daar enigiets goedkoper?** *Ihs dahr eniche·eets chuud·koo·per?*
When's checkout?	**Wanneer boek ek uit?** *Vahn·ny·eer book ack uyt?*

Visitors can expect an excellent choice of accomodations, from five-star hotels to modest city guesthouses, motorway motels, tranquil country inns, rustic **rondavels** (mud and wattle thatched huts) to luxury safari tents in game reserves. Camping is also well catered for and there is a superb selection of private hostels.

Can I leave this in the safe?	**Kan ek hierdie in die kluis los?**
	Cunn ack hier•dee ihn dee klays lohs?
Can I leave my bags?	**Kan ek my sakke los?**
	Cunn ack may suck•ke lohs?
Can I have my bill/ a receipt?	**Kan ek my rekening/'n kwitansie kry?** *Cunn ack may ree•kih•ning/ih kwih•tahn•see kray?*
I'll pay in cash/ by credit card.	**Ek sal in kontant/met kredietkaart betaal.** *Ack sahl ihn kawn•tant/meht krih•diet•kaart bih•taal.*

Communications

Where's an internet cafe?	**Waar's 'n internet kafee?**
	Vaahr's ih in•tir•net kha•feeh?
Can I access the internet/check my email?	**Kan ek toegang tot die internet verkry/my e-pos kyk?** *Cunn ack too•chang taut dee in•tir•net fir•kray/ may ee•paws kayk?*
How much per half hour/hour?	**Hoeveel per halfuur/uur?** *Who•feel per half•uhr/uhr.*
How do I connect/ log on?	**Hoe konnekteer ek/teken ek aan?** *Who kahwn• neck•tear ack/tee•kin ack aahn?*
A phone card, please.	**'n Foonkaart, asseblief.**
	ih Foon•kaart, us•sih•bleaf.

Can I have your phone number?	**Kan ek jou telefoonnommer kry?** *Cunn ack yi•oh*	
	tali•foon•nawm•mer kray?	
Here's my number/email.	**Hier's my nommer/epos.**	
	Hee•rs may nawm•mir/ee•paws.	
Call me/text me.	**Bel my/sms my.**	
	Bell may/es•em•es may	
I'll text you.	**Ek sal jou sms.**	
	Ack sull yi•oh es•em•es	
Email me.	**E•pos my.**	
	Ee•paws may.	
Hello. This is…	**Hallo. Dit is…**	
	Hell•oh. Diht ihs…	
Can I speak to…?	**Kan ek met….praat?**	
	Cunn ack met…praat?	
Can you repeat that?	**Kan jy dit herhaal?**	
	Cunn yay dit hehr•haal?	
I'll call back later.	**Ek sal later terugbel.**	
	Ack sull laah•tir tih•ruch•bell.	
Bye.	**Totsiens.** *Taut•seens.*	

South Africa is well•wired, with free WiFi services or dedicated computers for guests to use in many cafés and hotels. It is also very easy and inexpensive to purchase a local SIM card or to hire a cell phone for the duration of your stay (you can get these at the airport upon arrival).

Where's the post office?	**Waar's die poskantoor?** *Vaahr's dee paws•cunn•toor?*
I'd like to send this to...	**Ek wil graag hierdie vir...stuur.** *Ack vill chraach heer•dee fir...stuur.*
Can I...?	**Kan ek...?** *Cunn ack...?*
access the internet	**toegang tot die internet kry** *too•chang taut dee ihn•tir•net kray*
check my email	**my e•pos kyk** *may ee•paws kayk*
print	**druk** *druhk*
plug in/charge my laptop/iPhone/iPad/BlackBerry?	**my skootrekenaar/iPhone/iPad/Blackberry inprop/laai?** *may skooht•ree•kih•naahr/i•Phone/i•Pad/Black•berry ihn•prawp/laai?*
access Skype?	**toegang tot Skype verkry?** *too•chang tawt Skype fir•kray?*
What is the WiFi password?	**Wat is die WiFi wagwoord?** *Vaht iss dee Wi•Fi vach•voord?*
Is the WiFi free?	**Is die WiFi gratis?** *Ihs dee Wi•Fi chrah•tis?*
Do you have bluetooth?	**Het jul bluetooth?** *Heht yul blue•tooth?*
Do you have a scanner?	**Het jul 'n skandeerder?** *Heht yul ih scunn•deer•dir?*

Social Media

Are you on Facebook/Twitter?	**Is jy op Facebook/Twitter?** *Ihs yay awp Face•book/Twit•ter?*
What's your username?	**Wat is jou gebruikersnaam?** *Vaht ihs yi•oh che•bruy•kihrs•naam?*
I'll add you as a friend.	**Ek sal jou byvoeg as 'n vriend.** *Ack sahl yi•oh bay•fooch ahs ih freent*
I'll follow you on Twitter.	**Ek sal jou op Twitter volg.** *Ek sahl yi•oh awp Twit•tir fawlch*
Are you following…?	**Volg jy….?** *Fawlch yay…?*
I'll put the pictures on Facebook/Twitter.	**Ek sal die foto's op Facebook/Twitter sit.** *Ack sull dee foo•two's awp Face•book/Twit•tir sit*
I'll tag you in the pictures.	**Ek sal jou in die foto's merk.** *Ack sull yi•oh ihn dee foo•two's merck*

Conversation

Hello!/Hi!	**Hallo!/Hey!** *Hell•oh!/Hay!*
How are you?	**Hoe gaan dit?** *Who chaan diht?*
Fine, thanks.	**Goed, dankie.** *Chuuht, dung•key.*
Excuse me!	**Ekskuus!** *Axe•kuus*
Do you speak English?	**Praat jy Engels?** *Praaht yay Aeng•ils?*
What's your name?	**Wat is jou naam?** *Vaht ihs yi•oh naahm?*
My name is…	**My naam is…** *May naahm ihs…*
Nice to meet you.	**Lekker om jou te ontmoet.** *Lack•kir om yi•oh tih ohnt•moot*

Where are you from?	**Waar kom jy vandaan?**
	Vaahr kom jy fun·daan?
I'm from the...	**Ek is van die...** *Ack ihs fun dee...*
U.K./U.S.A.	**VK/VSA.** *Fee·Kah/Fee·Es·Aah*
What do you do for a living?	**Wat doen jy vir 'n lewe?**
	Vaht doon yay fir ih lee·vih?
I work for...	**Ek werk vir...** *Ack verk fir...*
I'm a student.	**Ek is 'n student.**
	Ack ihs ih stoo·dent
I'm retired.	**Ek is afgetree.**
	Ack ihs af·che·triyee

Romance

Would you like to go out for a drink/dinner?	**Wil jy vir 'n drankie/ete gaan?** *Vil yay fir ih drung· kye/eetih chaan?*
What are your plans for tonight/tomorrow?	**Wat is jou planne vir vanaand/môre?** *Vat ihs yi·oh plahn·nih fir fa·naant/more·ih?*
Can I have your (phone) number?	**Kan ek jou nommer kry?** *Cunn ack yi·oh nawm·mer kray?*
Can I join you?	**Kan ek by jou aansluit?** *Cunn ack bay yi·oh aan·slate?*
Can I buy you a drink?	**Kan ek vir jou 'n drankie koop?** *Cunn ack fir yi·oh ih drung·key ku·oop?*
I love you.	**Ek is lief vir jou.** *Ack ihs leaf fir yi·oh*

Accepting & Rejecting

I'd love to.	**Ek sal graag wil.**
	Ack sull chraach vill
Where should we meet?	**Waar moet ons ontmoet?**
	Vaahr moot awhns awnt•moot?
I'll meet you at the bar/your hotel.	**Ek sal jou by die kroeg/jou hotel ontmoet.**
	Ack sal yi•oh by die kroeg/yi•oh ho•tel ont•moet
I'll come by at…	**Ek sal teen…kom.**
	Ack sull tiyeen…kohm
I'm busy.	**Ek is besig.**
	Ack is biyee•sich
I'm not interested.	**Ek stel nie belang nie.**
	Ack stel•nie be•lung nie
Leave me alone.	**Los my uit.** *Laws may uayt*
Stop bothering me!	**Hou op om my te pla!**
	Hoe awp awm may tih plaah!

Food & Drink

Eating Out

Can you recommend a good restaurant/bar?	**Kan jy 'n goeie restaurant/kroeg aanbeveel?** *Cunn yay ih choei•e re•stau•rant/krooch aahn•bih•feehl?*
Is there a traditional/an inexpensive restaurant nearby?	**Is daar 'n tradisionele/'n goedkoop restaurant naby?** *Ihs daahr ih trah•dea•shio•nee•lih/ih chuud•koop res•tauw•runt nah•bay?*
A table for..., please.	**'n Tafel vir.... asseblief.** *ih Tah•fil fir....us•sih•bleaf*
Can we sit...?	**Kan ons....sit?** *Cunn ohns....sit?*
here/there	**hier/daar** *heer/daahr*
outside	**buite** *bay•tih*
in a non-smoking area	**in 'n nie•rookarea.** *ihn ih knee•ruhik•ahrea.*
I'm waiting for someone.	**Ek wag vir iemand.** *Ack vach fir ee•muhnt*
Where are the toilets?	**Waar is die toilette?** *Vaahr ihs dee toy•let•tih?*
The menu, please.	**Die spyskaart asseblief.** *Dee space•kaart us•sih•bleaf*
What do you recommend?	**Wat beveel jy aan?** *Vaht bih•feal yay aan?*
I'd like...	**Ek soek...** *Ack sook...*

There's something to suit all tastes and budgets in South Africa, especially in the larger cities where practically all global cuisines are represented.

Some more…, please.	**Bietjie meer …, asseblief.** *Bee·key mear…, us·sih·bleaf*
Enjoy your meal!	**Geniet jou ete!** *Che·neat yi·oh ee·tih!*
The check [bill], please.	**Die rekening, asseblief.** *Dee riye·kih·nihng, us·sih·bleaf*
Is service included?	**Is diens ingesluit?** *Ihs deance ihn·chih·slate?*
Can I pay by credit card/have a receipt?	**Kan ek met kredietkaart betaal/'n kwitansie kry?** *Cunn ack met krih·deet·kaart bih·taal/ih quit·an·sea kray?*

YOU MAY SEE…

INGANGSKOSTE	cover charge
VASGESTELDE PRYS	fixed price
SPYSKAART (VAN DIE DAG)	menu (of the day)
DIENS (NIE) INGESLUIT	service (not) included
SPESIALE AANBIEDINGS	specials

Breakfast

Bacon	**spek** *speck*
Bread	**brood** *bruh·oot*
butter	**botter** *bawt·tir*
cold cuts	**koue snye vleis** *kow·ih snay·ih flace*
cheese	**kaas** *kaas*
egg	**eier** *ay·ihr*
hard/soft boiled	**hard/saggekook** *hart/sach·che·kuook*
fried	**gebak** *che·buck*
scrambled	**geroer** *che·ruur*
jam/jelly	**konfyt/jellie** *kawn·fate/jel·lee*
omelet	**ommelet** *ohm·mih·let*
toast	**roosterbrood** *ru·oos·ter·brood*
sausage	**worsie** *vhor·see*
yogurt	**jogurt** *yo·chirt*

From hearty Dutch cooking with subtle Malay influences to Indian curries and traditional African stews, the national cuisine is a delicious mix.

Appetizers

Pâté	**Patee** *Pah•tyee*	
Fish soup	**Vissop** *Fiss•sawp*	
Vegetable/tomato soup	**Groente/tamatiesop** *Chrune•tih/tah•mah•tea•sawp*	
Chicken soup	**Hoendersop** *Huun•dir•sawp*	
Salad	**Slaai** *Slai*	

> **YOU MAY HEAR...**
>
> **rou** *row*   Rare
> **medium** *me•dee•uhm*   Medium
> **gaar** *chaar*   Well-done

Meat

Beef	**Bief** *Beef*
Chicken	**Hoender** *Huun•dir*
Lamb	**Lam** *Lumm*

Pork	**Vark** *Fark*
Steak	**Biefstuk** *Beef•stik*
Veal	**Wild** *Vild*

Fish & Seafood

Cod	**Kabeljou** *Kaa•bil•yi•oh*
Fishcakes	**viskoekies** *Fis•koo•keys*
Herring	**Haring** *Ha•ring*
Lobster	**kreef** *kryeef*
salmons	**salm** *salim*
Shrimp [prawns]	**Garnale** *Char•nah•lih*

Vegetables

Beans	**Boontjies** *Boon•keys*
Cabbage	**Kool** *Quool*
Carrots	**Wortels** *Vor•tils*
Mushroom	**Sampioen** *Sum•pee•uun*
Onion	**Uie** *Uy•e*
Peas	**Ertjies** *Aer•keys*

| Potato | **Aartappel** *Are·tupp·pil* |
| Tomato | **Tamatie** *Tah·mah·tee* |

Sauces & Condiments

Salt	**Sout** *Souwt*
Pepper	**Peper** *Pe·pir*
Mustard	**Mosterd** *Moss·tird*
Ketchup	**Tamatiesous** *Tah·maa·tee·sous*

Fruit & Dessert

Apple	**Appel** *Ahp·pil*
Banana	**Piesang** *Pee·sung*
Lemon	**Suurlemoen** *Suur·lih·moon*

A popular snack throughout South Africa is **biltong**, air-dried strips of salted and spiced meat similiar to American jerky. It is often made with beef or ostrich, but true connoisseurs favour venison, in particular **kudu** or **springbok**.

Orange	**Lemoen** *Lih•moon*
Pear	**Peer** *Peer*
Strawberries	**Aarbeie** *Aahr•bay•ih*
ice cream	**Roomys** *ruoom•ace*
chocolate/vanilla	**sjokolade/vanilla** *shoh•kih•lah•dih/vah•nil•lah*
tart/cake	**tert/koek** *terht/cook*
mousse	**mousse** *mousse*
custard/cream	**vla/room** *fla/ruoom*

Drinks

The wine list/drink menu, please.	**Die wynlys/dranklys, asseblief.** *Dee vayne•lace/ drungk•lace, us•sih•bleaf.*
What do you recommend?	**Wat beveel jy aan?** *Vaht bih•feel yay aan?*
I'd like a bottle/glass of red/white wine.	**Ek soek 'n bottel/glas rooi/wit wyn.** *Ack sook ih bawt•til/chlas ruoi/vit vayne.*
The house wine, please.	**Die huiswyn, asseblief.** *Dee huys•vayne, us•sih•bleaf.*
Another bottle/glass, please.	**Nog 'n bottel/glas, asseblief.** *Noch ih bawt•til/chlas, us•sih•bleaf.*

Cabarnet sauvignon is the most-widely planted red in the Cape, and it tends to produce heavy wines that are ideal with steak and red meats. Pinotage is a good value South African cultivar, developed from a cross between Pino Noir and Cinsaut.
As for whites, Chenin Blanc and Columbard dominate while Sauvignon Blanc is gaining popularity. Chardonnay is the priciest and most popular in the region.

I'd like a local beer.	**Ek soek 'n plaaslike bier.**
	Ack soek 'n plaas•li•ke bier.
Can I buy you a drink?	**Kan ek vir jou 'n drankie koop?**
	Cunn ack fir yi•oh ih drung•key kuoop?
Cheers!	**Gesondheid!** *Che•sawnd•hate!*
A coffee/tea, please.	**'n koffie/tee, asseblief.**
	ih kawf•fee/tyee, us•sih•bleaf.
Black.	**Swart.** *Suart*
With...	**Met...** *met*
milk	**melk** *melck*
sugar	**suiker** *suy•kir*
artificial sweetener	**kunsmatige versoeter**
	kihns•mah•tih•che fir•soo•tir
A..., please.	**'n..., asseblief.** *ih..., us•sih•bleaf.*
juice	**sap** *supp*
soda [soft drink]	**soda** *soo•dah*
(sparkling/still)	**water** *vah•tir*
water	

Leisure Time

Sightseeing

Where's the tourist information office?	**Waar is die inligtingskantoor?** *Vaahr ihs dee ihn·lich·tings·cunn·toohr?*
What are the main sights?	**Wat is die hoof besienswaardighede?** *Vaht ihs dee whiff bih·seens·vaar·dich·yedih?*
Do you offer tours in English?	**Bied julle toere in Engels aan?** *Beat yul·lih tu·rih ihn Aeng·ils aan?*
Can I have a map/guide?	**Kan ek 'n kaart/gids kry?** *Cunn ack ih kaart/chids kray?*

For Eating Out, see page 130.

A trip to South Africa would not be complete without a visit to Kruger National Park which hosts some of the world's highest concentrations of animals, including lions, elephants, zebra, giraffe, leopards and rhinos. Visit **www.sanparks.org** for more information.

Shopping

Where's the market/mall?	**Waar is die mark/winkelsentrum?**	*Vaahr ihs dee mark/ving•kil•sen•trim?*
I'm just looking.	**Ek kyk net.**	*Ack kayk net.*
Can you help me?	**Kan jy my help?**	*Cunn yay may help*
I'm being helped.	**Ek word gehelp.**	*Ack vord che•help.*
How much?	**Hoeveel?**	*Who•fiyeel?*
That one, please.	**Daardie een, asseblief.**	*Daahr•dee een, us•sih•bleaf.*
I'd like…	**Ek soek….**	*Ack sook…*
That's all.	**Dis al.**	*Dihs ahl.*
Where can I pay?	**Waar kan ek betaal?**	*Vaahr cunn ack bih•taahl?*
I'll pay in cash/by credit card.	**Ek sal met kontant/met kredietkaart betaal.**	*Ack sull met kawn•tant/met krih•deat•kaart bih•taahl.*
A receipt, please.	**'n Kwitansie asseblief.**	*ih Quit•an•see us•sih•bleaf.*

YOU MAY SEE…

OOP/TOE	open/closed
INGANG/UITGANG	entrance/exit

Sport & Leisure

When's the game?	**Waaneer is die wedstryd?** *Vaahn•eer ihs dee vehd•strait?*
Where's…?	**Waar is…?** *Vaahr ihs….?*
the beach	**die strand** *dee strahnt*
the park	**die park** *dee park*
the pool	**die swembad** *dee su•wem•bad*
Is it safe to swim here?	**Is dit veilig om hier te swem?** *Ihs dit fay•lich awm hier tih su•wem?*
Can I hire clubs?	**Kan ek stokke huur?** *Cunn ack stawk•kih huur?*
How much per hour/day?	**Hoe baie is dit per uur/dag?** *Who bye•ih ihs dit per uhr/dach?*
How far is it to…?	**Hoe ver is dit na…?** *Who fer ihs dit nah…?*

Going Out

What's there to do at night?	**Wat kan mens in die aand doen?** *Vaht cunn mens ihn dee aand doon?*
Do you have a program of events?	**Het jy 'n program van gebeure?** *Het yay ih pru•chram fun che•bee•yu•rih?*
What's playing tonight?	**Wat speel vanaand?** *Vaht spyeel fun•aant?*

Where's…?	**Waar's…?** *Vaahr's…?*
the downtown area	**die dorpsarea** *dee dohrps•aa•reeya*
the bar	**die kroeg** *dee krooch*
the dance club	**die dansklub** *dee daans•club*
Is this area safe at night?	**Is hierdie area veilig in die aand?** *Ihs heer•dee aa• reeya fay•lich ihn dee aant?*

Baby Essentials

Do you have…?	**Het jy….?** *Heht yay…?*
a baby bottle	**'n baba bottel** *ih baa•baa boht•til*
baby food	**baba kos** *baa•baa kaws*
baby wipes	**baba doeke** *baa•baa doo•kih*
a car seat	**'n karstoeltjie** *ih kahr•stool•key*
a children's menu/ portion	**'n kinder spyskaart/porsie** *ih kin•dir space•cart/ pour•see*
a child's seat/ highchair	**'n kinderstoeltjie/hoë stoel** *ih kin•dir•stool•key/ who•ih stool*
a crib/cot	**'n wiegie/kot** *ih vee•chee/kawt*
diapers [nappies]	**doeke** *doo•kih*
formula	**formule** *for•muh•lih*
a pacifier [dummy]	**'n fopspeen** *ih fohp•spiyeen*

a playpen	**'n speelkampie** *ih spiyeel•kahm•pee*
a stroller [pushchair]	**'n stootkarretjie** *ih stuoot•kahr•ree•key*
Can I breastfeed the baby here?	**Kan ek my baba hier borsvoed?** *Cunn ack may baa•baa hiir bawrs•fud?*
Where can I breastfeed/change the baby?	**Waar kan ek my baba borsvoed?** *Vaahr cunn ack may baa•baa bawrs•fud?*

Disabled Travelers

Is there…?	**Is daar…?** *Ihs daahr…?*
access for the disabled	**toegang vir die gestremde** *too•chang fir dee chih•strehm•dih*
a wheelchair ramp	**'n rystoel oprit** *ih ray•stool ohp•rit*
a disabled-accessible toilet	**'n toeganklike toilet vir die gestremde** *ih too•changk•lihkih toy•let fir dee che•strem•dih*
I need…	**Ek kort…** *Ack court*
assistance	**hulp…** *huhlp*
an elevator [a lift]	**'n hysbak** *ih hayce•buck*
a ground-floor room	**'n kamer op grondvloer** *ih kah•mir awp chrawnd•fluur*
Please speak louder.	**Praat asseblief harder.** *Praat us•sih•bleaf har•dir*

Health & Emergencies

Emergencies

Help!	**Help!** *Help!*	
Go away!	**Gaan weg!** *Chaan vech!*	
Stop, thief!	**Stop, dief!** *Stawp, deef!*	
Get a doctor!	**Kry 'n dokter!**	
	Kray ih dawk•tir!	
Fire!	**Brand!** *Brunt!*	
I'm lost.	**Ek's verdwaal/verlore.**	
	Axe fir•duwaal/fir•luoo•rih.	
Can you help me?	**Kan jy my help?**	
	Cunn yay may help?	
Call the police!	**Bel die polisie!**	
	Bell dee pooh•lee•see!	
Where's the police station?	**Waar is die polisiestasie?** *Vaahr ihs dee pooh•lee•see•stah•see?*	
My child is missing.	**My kind word vermis.**	
	May kind vohrd fir•mis.	

YOU MAY HEAR...

Vul hierdie vorm in. *Fil heer•dee forim ihn*	Fill out this form.
Jou ID, asseblief. *Yi•oh ee•diyee, us•sih•bleaf*	Your ID, please.
Wanneer/Waar het dit gebeur? *Vahn•niyeer/Vaahr heht dit che•bee•yur?*	When/Where did it happen?
Hoe lyk hy/sy? *Who lake hay/say?*	What does he/she look like?

Health

I'm sick.	**Ek is siek.** *Ack ihs seek.*
I need an English-speaking doctor.	**Ek benodig 'n Engelssprekende dokter.** *Ack bih‧nuoo‧dich ih Aeng‧ils‧spree‧kin‧dih dawk‧tir*
It hurts here.	**Dit is seer hier.** *Diht ihs siyeer hiir*
Where's the pharmacy?	**Waar is die apteek?** *Vaahr ihs dee ahp‧tiyeek?*
I'm (...months) pregnant.	**Ek is .... maande swanger.** *Ack ihs .... maahn‧dih suwanger*
I'm on...	**Ek's op...** *Axe awp...*
I'm allergic to antibiotics/penicillin.	**Ek's allergies vir** *Axe ah‧ler‧gies vir* **anti‧biotika/Penisillien** *ahn‧tea‧bee‧yo‧tea‧kah/peh‧nih‧sill‧leen*

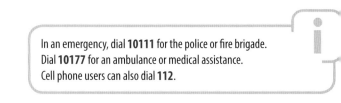

In an emergency, dial **10111** for the police or fire brigade.
Dial **10177** for an ambulance or medical assistance.
Cell phone users can also dial **112**.

Dictionary

acetaminophen [paracetamol] 'n asetaminofien [parasetamol]

adaptor 'n aansluitprop

aid worker hulpwerker

and en

antiseptic cream anti-septiese room

aspirin aspirien

baby baba

a backpack 'n rugsak

bad sleg

bag sak

Band-Aid [plasters] Pleister

bandages verbande

battleground slagveld

bee by

beige beige

bikini tweestuk

bird voël

black swart

bland (food) doodgewone (kos)

blue blou

bottle opener botteloopmaker

bowl bakkie

boy seun

boyfriend kêrel

bra bra

brown bruin

camera kamera

can opener blikoopmaker

cat kat

castle kasteel

charger laaier

cigarettes sigarette

cold koud

comb (n) kam

computer rekenaar

condoms kondome

contact lens solution kontaklensoplossing

corkscrew kurktrekker

cup koppie

dangerous gevaarlik

deodorant reukweerder

diabetic diabeet

dog hond

doll pop

fly n vlieg

fork vurk

girl dogter

girlfriend meisie

glass glas

good goed

gray grys

great goed

green groen

a hairbrush 'n haarborsel

hairspray haarsproei

horse perd
hot warm
husband man
ibuprofen ibuprofeen
ice ys
icy ysig
injection inspuiting
I'd like… Ek soek…
insect repellent insekweerder
jeans jeans
(steak) knife (biefstuk)mes
lactose intolerant laktose-
   intollerant
large groot
lighter aansteker
lion leeu
lotion [moisturizing cream] room
love liefde
matches vuurhoutjies
medium medium
monkey apie
museum museum
my my
nail file 'n naelvyl
napkin 'n servet
nurse verpleegster
or of
orange oranje
park parkie
partner metgesel/vennoot
pen pen

pink pienk
plate bord
purple pers
pyjamas pajamas/nagklere
rain reën
a raincoat 'n reënjas
a (disposable) razor 'n
   (weggooibare) skeermes
razor blades skeermeslemmetjies
red rooi
safari safari
salty souterig
sandals sandale
sanitary napkins [pads] sanitêre
   doekies
scissors skêr
shampoo/conditioner sjampoe/
   opknapper
shoes skoene
small klein
snake slang
sneakers seilskoene
snow sneeu
soap seep
socks sokkies
spicy kruierig
spider spinnekop
spoon lepel
a sweater 'n sweetpak
stamp(s) seëls
suitcase tas

sun son
sunglasses sonbrille
sunscreen sonskerm
a sweatshirt 'n sweetpakbaadjie
a swimsuit 'n swembroek
a T-shirt 'n T-hemp
tampons tampons
terrible aaklig
tie das
tissues sneesdoekies
toilet paper toiletpapier
toothbrush tandeborsel
toothpaste tandepasta
tough (meat) taai
toy speelding
underwear onderklere
vegetarian vegetaries
vegan vegan
white wit
with met
wife vrou
without sonder
yellow geel
your jou
zoo dieretuin

French

Essentials

Hello.	**Bonjour.** *bohN·zhoor*
Goodbye.	**Au revoir.** *oh ruh·vwahr*
Yes.	**Oui.** *wee*
No.	**Non.** *nohN*
OK.	**D'accord.** *dah·kohr*
Excuse me! (to get attention)	**Excusez-moi!** *ehk·skew·zay·mwah*
Excuse me. (to get past)	**Pardon.** *pahr·dohN*
I'm sorry.	**Je suis désolé** *m* **/désolée** *f zhuh swee day·zoh·lay*
I'd like…	**Je voudrais…** *zhuh voo·dray…*
How much?	**Combien ça coûte?** *kohN·beeyehN sah koot*
And/Or.	**Et/Ou.** *eh/oo*
Where is…?	**Où est…?** *oo ay…*
Please.	**S'il vous plaît.** *seel voo play*
Thank you.	**Merci.** *mehr·see*
You're welcome.	**De rien.** *duh reeyehN*
I'm going to…	**Je vais à/aux…** *zhuh vay ah/oh…*
My name is…	**Mon nom est…** *mohN nohN ay…*
Please speak slowly.	**S'il vous plaît, parlez lentement.** *seel voo play pahr·lay lawN·tuh·mawN*
Can you repeat that?	**Pouvez-vous répéter cela?** *poo·vay·voo ray·pay·tay suh·lah*
I don't understand.	**Je ne comprends pas.** *zhuh nuh kohN·prawN pah*
Do you speak English?	**Parlez-vous anglais?** *pahr·lay·voo awN·glay*
I don't speak French.	**Je ne parle pas français.** *zhuh nuh pahrl pah frawN·say*
Where's the restroom [toilet]?	**Où sont les toilettes?** *oo sohN lay twah·leht*
Help!	**Au secours !** *oh suh·koohr*

You'll find the pronunciation of the French letters and words written in gray after each sentence to guide you. Simply pronounce these as if they were English. As you hear the language being spoken, you will quickly become accustomed to the local pronunciation and dialect. Note that the vocabulary and terminology can vary depending on your destination but standard French is taught in schools, is used in all media and official documents.

Numbers

0	**zéro**	*zay•roh*
1	**un**	*uhN*
2	**deux**	*duh*
3	**trois**	*trwah*
4	**quatre**	*kah•truh*
5	**cinq**	*sehNk*
6	**six**	*sees*
7	**sept**	*seht*
8	**huit**	*weet*

9	**neuf**	
	nuhf	
10	**dix**	
	dees	
11	**onze**	
	ohNz	
12	**douze**	
	dooz	
13	**treize**	
	trehz	
14	**quatorze**	
	kah•tohrz	
15	**quinze**	
	kehNz	
16	**seize**	
	sehz	
17	**dix-sept**	
	dee•seht	
18	**dix-huit**	
	deez•weet	
19	**dix-neuf**	
	deez•nuhf	
20	**vingt**	
	vehN	
21	**vingt-et-un**	
	vehN•tay•uhN	
22	**vingt-deux**	
	vehN•duh	
30	**trente**	
	trawNt	

31	**trente-et-un**	*trawN·tay·uhN*
40	**quarante**	*kah·rawNt*
50	**cinquante**	*sehN·kawNt*
60	**soixante**	*swah·zawNt*
70	**soixante-dix**	*swah·zawNt·dees*
80	**quatre-vingt**	*kah·truh·vehN*
90	**quatre-vingt-dix**	*kah·truh·vehN·dees*
100	**cent**	*sawN*
101	**cent-un**	*sawN·uhN*
200	**deux-cent**	*duh·sawN*
500	**cinq-cent**	*sehNk·sawN*
1,000	**mille**	*meel*
10,000	**dix mille**	*dee meel*
1,000,000	**un million**	*uhN meel·yohN*

Time

What time is it?	**Quelle heure est-il?**
	kehl uhr ay•teel
It's midday.	**Il est midi.**
	ee lay mee•dee
Five past three.	**Trois heures cinq.**
	trwah zuhr sehNk
A quarter to ten.	**Dix heures moins le quart.**
	dee zuhr mwehN luh kahr
5:30 a.m./p.m.	**Cinq heures et demie du matin/de l'après-midi.**
	sehN kuhr eh duh•mee dew mah•tehN/ duh lah•preh•mee•dee

Days

Monday	**lundi**
	luhN•dee
Tuesday	**mardi**
	mahr•dee
Wednesday	**mercredi**
	mehr•kruh•dee
Thursday	**jeudi**
	zhuh•dee
Friday	**vendredi**
	vawN•druh•dee
Saturday	**samedi**
	sahm•dee
Sunday	**dimanche**
	dee•mawNsh

Dates

yesterday	**hier**
	eeyehr
today	**aujourd'hui**
	oh•zhoor•dwee
tomorrow	**demain**
	duh•mehN
day	**le jour**
	luh zhoor
week	**la semaine**
	lah suh•mehN
month	**le mois**
	luh mwah
year	**l'année/l'an**
	lah•nay/lawN
Happy New Year!	**Bonne année !**
	bohN ah•nay
Happy Birthday!	**Joyeux anniversaire !**
	zhoy•uhz ah•nee•vehr•sehr

For Numbers, see page 150.

Months

January	**janvier** *zhawN·veeyay*
February	**février** *fay·vreeyay*
March	**mars** *mahrs*
April	**avril** *ah·vreel*
May	**mai** *may*
June	**juin** *zhwehN*
July	**juillet** *zhwee·yay*
August	**août** *oot*
September	**septembre** *sehp·tawN·bruh*
October	**octobre** *ohk·toh·bruh*
November	**novembre** *noh·vawN·bruh*
December	**décembre** *day·sawN·bruh*

Arrival & Departure

I'm on vacation [holiday]/business.	**Je suis en vacances/voyage d'affaires.** *zhuh swee zawN vah·kawNs/vwah·yahzh dah·fehr*
I'm going to...	**Je vais à/aux...** *zhuh vay ah/oh...*
I'm staying at the...Hotel.	**Je reste à l'hôtel...** *zhuh rehst ah loh·tehl...*

You will find French speakers in the Central African Republic, the Congo, Chad, Rwanda, Gabon, among others. Most foreign visitors are here for work, with the expetion of Rwanda and gorilla safaris.

Money

Where's…?	**Où est…?** *oo ay…*
the ATM	**le distributeur automatique de billets**
	luh dee•stree•bew•tuhr oh•toh•mah•teek duh bee•yay
the bank	**la banque** *lah bawNk*
the currency exchange office	**le bureau de change**
	luh bew•roh duh shawNzh
When does the bank open/close?	**Quand est-ce que la banque ouvre/ferme?**
	kawN tehs kuh lah bawNk oo•vruh/fehrm
I'd like to change dollars/pounds/euros into …	**Je voudrais échanger des dollars/livres/euros sterling en …** *zhuh voo•dray ay•shawN•zhay*
	day doh•lahr/lee•vruh stayr•leeng/ nuh•roh awN…
I'd like to cash traveler's cheques.	**Je voudrais encaisser des chèques de voyages.**
	zhuh voo•dray awN•kay•say day shehk duh vwah•yahzh
Can I pay by cash?	**Je peux payer en espèces?**
	zhuh puh pay•yay awN nehs•pehs?
Can I pay by credit card?	**Puis-je payer par carte?**
	pwee•zhuh pay•yay pahr kahrt

YOU MAY SEE…

The **Central African Franc (CFA)** is the currency in six countries: Cameroon, Central African Republic, Chad, Republic of the Congo, Equatorial Guinea and Gabon. Note that this cannot be interchanged with the CFA in West Africa. If traveling to other French-speaking destinations, check the local currrency before you travel.

Getting Around

How do I get to town?	**Comment vais-je en ville?** *koh•mawN vay•zhuh awN veel*
Where's…?	**Où est…?** *oo ay…*
the airport	**l'aéroport** *lah•ay•roh•pohr*
the train station	**la gare** *lah gahr*
the bus station	**la gare routière** *lah gahr roo•tee•yehr*
Is it far from here?	**C'est loin d'ici?** *say lwehN dee•see*
Where do I buy a ticket?	**Où puis-je acheter un billet?** *oo pwee•zhuh a ah•shtay uhN bee•yay*
A one-way/return-trip ticket to…	**Un billet aller simple/aller-retour…** *uhN bee•yay ah•lay sehN•pluh/ah•lay•ruh•toor…*
How much?	**Combien ça coûte?** *kohN•beeyehN sah koot*
Which gate/line?	**Quelle porte/ligne?** *kehl pohrt/lee•nyuh*
Which platform?	**Quel quai?** *kehl kay*
Where can I get taxi?	**Où puis-je prendre un taxi?** *oo pwee•zhuh a prawN•druh uhN tahk•see*
Take me to this address.	**Conduisez-moi à cette adresse.** *kohN•dwee•zay•mwah ah seh tah•drehs*
To…Airport, please.	**À l'aéroport de…, s'il vous plaît.** *ah lah•ay•roh•pohr duh…seel voo play*
I'm in a rush.	**Je suis pressé m/pressée f.** *zhuh swee preh•say*
Can I have a map?	**Puis-je avoir une carte?** *pwee•zhuh ah•vwahr ewn kahrt*

Tickets

When's…to Bangui?	**Quand est…pour Bangui?** *kawN tay…poor Ban•gwee*
the (first) bus	**le (premier) bus** *luh (pruh•meeyay) bews*
the (next) flight	**le (prochain) vol** *luh (proh•shehN) vohl*
the (last) train	**le (dernier) train** *luh (dehr•neeyay) trehN*
One/Two ticket(s).	**Un/Deux billet(s).** *uhN/duh bee•yay*
For today/tomorrow.	**Pour aujourd'hui/demain.** *poor oh•zhoor•dwee/duh•mehN*
A…ticket.	**Un billet…** *uhN bee•yay…*
one-way	**aller simple** *nah•lay sehN•pluh*
return trip	**aller-retour** *nah•lay•ruh•toor*
first class	**première classe** *pruh•meeyehr klahs*
I have an e-ticket.	**J'ai un billet électronique.** *zhay uhN bee•yay ay•lehk•troh•neek*
How long is the trip?	**Combien de temps dure le voyage?** *kohN• beeyehN duh tawN dewr luh vwah•yahzh*
Is it a direct train?	**Est-ce que c'est un train direct?** *ehs kuh say tuhN trehN dee•rehkt*
Is this the bus to…?	**Est-ce le bus pour…?** *ehs luh bews poor…*
Can you tell me when to get off?	**Pouvez-vous me dire quand je dois descendre?** *poo•vay•voo muh deer kawN zhuh dwah deh•sawN•druh*
I'd like to…	**Je voudrais…ma réservation.** *zhuh voo•dray…mah ray•zehr•vah•seeyohN*
my reservation.	
cancel	**annuler** *ah•new•lay*
change	**échanger** *ay•shawN•zhay*
confirm	**confirmer** *kohN•feer•may*

For Time, see page 153.

Car Hire

Where's the car hire?	**Où est l'agence de location de voitures?** *oo ay lah·zhawNs duh loh·kah·seeyohN duh vwah·tewr*
I'd like…	**Je voudrais…** *zhuh voo·dray…*
a cheap/small car	**une voiture bon marché/petite voiture** *ewn vwah·tewr bohN mahr·shay/puh·teet vwah·tewr*
an automatic/ a manual	**une automatique/manuelle** *ewn oh·toh·mah·teek/mah·new·ehl*
air conditioning	**la climatisation** *lah klee·mah·tee·zah·seeyohN*
a car seat	**un siège bébé** *uhN seeyehzh bay·bay*
How much…?	**Combien ça coûte…?** *kohN·beeyehN sah koot…*
per day/week	**par jour/semaine** *pahr zhoor/suh·mehN*
Are there any discounts?	**Y-a-t-il des réductions?** *yah·teel day ray·dewk·seeyohN*

YOU MAY HEAR…

tout droit *too drwah*	straight ahead
à gauche *ah gohsh*	left
à droite *ah drwaht*	right
au coin *oh kwehN*	around the corner
à l'opposé *ah loh·poh·zay*	opposite
derrière *deh·reeyehr*	behind
près de *pray duh*	next to
après *ah·pray*	after
nord/sud *nohr/sewd*	north/south
est/ouest *ehst/oowehst*	east/west
au feu (tricolore) *oh fuh (tree·koh·lohr)*	at the traffic light
au carrefour *oh cahr·foor*	at the intersection

Places to Stay

Essentials

Can you recommend a hotel?	**Pouvez-vous me conseiller un hôtel?** *poo•vay•voo muh kohN•say•yay uhN noh•tehl*
I made a reservation.	**J'ai fait une réservation.** *zhay fay ewn ray•zehr•vah•seeyohN*
My name is...	**Mon nom est...** *mohN nohN ay...*
Do you have a room...?	**Avez-vous une chambre...?** *ah•vay•voo ewn shawN•bruh...*
for one/two	**pour un/deux** *poor uhN/duh*
with a bathroom	**avec salle de bains** *ah•vehk sahl duh behN*
with air conditioning	**avec climatisation** *ah•vehk klee•mah•tee•zah•seeyohN*
For...	**Pour...** *poor...*
tonight	**ce soir** *suh swahr*
two nights	**deux nuits** *duh nwee*
one week	**une semaine** *ewn suh•mehn*
How much?	**Combien ça coûte?** *kohN•beeyehN sah koot*

160

Is there anything cheaper?	**N'y-a-t-il rien de moins cher?** *Nee•yah•teel reeyehN duh mwehN shehr*
When's check-out?	**Quand dois-je quitter la chambre?** *kawN dwah•zhuh kee•tay lah shawN•bruh*
Can I leave this in the safe?	**Puis-je laisser ceci dans le coffre?** *pwee•zhuh lay•say suh•see dawN luh koh•fruh*
Can I leave my bags?	**Puis-je laisser mes bagages?** *pwee•zhuh lay•say meh bah•gahzh*
Can I have my bill/ a receipt?	**Puis-je avoir ma facture/un reçu?** *pwee•zhuh ah•vwahr mah fahk•tewr/uhN ruh•sew*
I'll pay in cash/by credit card.	**Je paierai en espèces/par carte de crédit.** *zhuh pay•ray awN nehs•pehs/pahr kahrt duh kray•dee*

Note that it is not easy to exchange worn U.S. dollars and you may need to travel to many different banks to be able to do this. The euro and pound sterling are also accepted in some places but again, this varies on where you are so it is advisable to research this before your trip.

Communications

Where's an internet cafe?	**Où y-a-t-il un cyber café?** *oo yah•teel uhN see•behr kah•fay*
Can I access the internet/check my e-mail?	**Puis-je me connecter à Internet/consulter mes mails?** *pwee•zhuh muh koh•nehk•tay ah ehN•tehr•neht/kohN•sewl•tay may mehyl*
How much per half hour/hour?	**Combien coûte la demi-heure/l'heure?** *kohN•beeyehN koot lah duh•mee•uhr/luhr*
How do I connect/log on?	**Comment est-ce que je me connecte/ j'ouvre une session?** *koh•mawN ehs kuh zhuh muh koh•nehkt/zhoo•vruh ewn seh•seeyohN*
A phone card, please.	**Une carte de téléphone, s'il vous plaît.** *ewn kahrt duh tay•lay•fohn seel voo play*
Can I have your phone number?	**Puis-je avoir votre numéro de téléphone?** *pwee•zhuh ah•vwahr voh•truh new•meh•roh duh tay•lay•fohn*
Here's my number/e-mail.	**Voici mon numéro/mail.** *vwah•see mohN new•meh•roh/mehyl*
Please call/text me.	**S'il vous plaît, appelez-moi/envoyez-moi un SMS.** *seel voo play ah•puh•lay•mwah/ awN•vwah•yay•mwah uhN ehs•ehm•ehs*
I'll call/text you.	**Je vous appellerai/enverrai un SMS.** *zhuh voo zah•peh•luh•ray/zawN•veh•ray uhN nehs•ehm•ehs*
E-mail me.	**Envoie-moi un mail.** *awN•vwah•mwah uhN mehyl*
Hello. This is...	**Bonjour. C'est...** *bohN•zhoor say...*
Can I speak to...?	**Puis-je parler à...?** *pwee•zhuh pahr•lay ah...*
Can you repeat that?	**Pouvez-vous répéter cela?** *poo•vay•voo ray•pay•tay suh•lah*
I'll call back later.	**Je rappellerai plus tard.** *zhuh rah•peh•luh•ray plew tahr*
Bye.	**Au revoir.** *oh ruh•vwahr*

Where's the post office?	**Où est la poste?** *oo ay lah pohst*
I'd like to send this to…	**Je voudrais envoyer ceci à…** *zhuh voo•dray zawN•vwah•yay suh•see ah…*
Can I…?	**Puis-je…?** *pwee•zhuh…*
access the internet	**accéder à Internet** *ahk•seh•day ah ehN•tehrneht*
check my email	**consulter mes mails** *kohN•sewl•tay may mehyl*
print	**imprimer** *ehN•pree•may*
plug in/charge my laptop/iPhone/ iPad/BlackBerry?	**brancher/charger mon ordinateur portable/ iPhone/iPad/Blackberry?** *brawN•shay/ shahr•zhay mohN nohr•dee•nah•tuhr pohr•tah•bluh/ ee•fohn/ee•pahd/black•ber•ee*
access Skype?	**accéder à Skype?** *ah•ksay•day ah skiep*
What is the WiFi password?	**Quel est le mot de passe du WiFi?** *keh lay luh moh duh pahs dew wee•fee*
Is the WiFi free?	**Est-ce que le WiFi est gratuit?** *ehs kuh luh wee•fee ay grah•twee*
Do you have bluetooth?	**Avez-vous Bluetooth?** *ah•vay•voo bloo•toohs*
Do you have a scanner?	**Avez-vous un scanneur?** *ah•vay•voo uhN skah•nuhr*

163

Social Media

Are you on Facebook/Twitter?	**Etes-vous sur Facebook/Twitter?** *(polite form)*
	eht•voo sewr fayhs•book/twee•teuhr
	Es-tu sur Facebook/Twitter? *(informal form)*
	eh•tew sewr fayhs•book/twee•teuhr
What's your user name?	**Quel est votre nom d'utilisateur?** *(polite form)*
	keh lay voh•truh nohN dew•tee•lee•zah•tuhr
	Quel est ton nom d'utilisateur? *(informal form)*
	keh lay tohN nohN dew•tee•lee•zah•tuhr
I'll add you as a friend.	**Je vous ajouterai comme ami.** *(polite form)*
	zhuh voo zah•zhoo•tray kohm ah•mee
	Je t'ajouterai comme ami. *(informal form)*
	zhuh tah•zhoo•tray kohm ah•mee
I'll follow you on Twitter.	**Je vous suivrai sur Twitter.** *(polite form)*
	zhuh voo swee•vray sewr twitter
	Je te suivrai sur Twitter. *(informal form)*
	zhuh tuh swee•vray sewr twitter
Are you following…?	**Suivez-vous…?** *(polite form)* *swee•vay voo*
	Suis-tu…? *(informal form)* *swee tew*
I'll put the pictures on Facebook/Twitter.	**Je mettrai les photos sur Facebook/Twitter.**
	zhuh may•tray lay foh•toh sewr fayhs•book/twee•teuhr
I'll tag you in the pictures.	**Je vous marquerai sur les photos.** *(polite form)*
	zhuh voo mahr•kuh•ray sewr lay foh•toh
	Je te marquerai sur les photos. *(informal form)*
	zhuh tuh mahr•kuh•ray sewr lay foh•toh

Conversation

Hello!/Hi!	**Bonjour!/Salut !**	*bohN·zhoor/sah·lew*
How are you?	**Comment allez-vous?**	*koh·mawN tah·lay·voo*
Fine, thanks.	**Bien, merci.**	*beeyehN mehr·see*
Excuse me!	**Excusez-moi !**	*ehk·skew·zay·mwah*
Do you speak English?	**Parlez-vous anglais?**	*pahr·lay·voo zawN·glay*
What's your name?	**Comment vous appelez-vous?**	*koh·mawN voo zah·puh·lay·voo*
My name is...	**Je m'appelle...**	*zhuh mah·pehl...*
Nice to meet you.	**Enchanté** *m*/**Enchantée** *f.*	*awN·shawN·tay*
Where are you from?	**D'où êtes-vous?**	*doo eht·voo*
I'm from the U.K./U.S.	**Je viens du Royaume-Uni/des États-Unis.**	*zhuh veeyehN dew rwah·yohm·ew·nee/ day zay·tah·zew·nee*
What do you do for a living?	**Que faites-vous dans la vie?**	*kuh feht·voo dawN lah vee*
I work for...	**Je travaille pour...**	*zhuh trah·vie poor...*
I'm a student.	**Je suis étudiant** *m*/**étudiante** *f.*	*zhuh swee zay·tew·deeyawN/zay·tew·deeyawnt*
I'm retired.	**Je suis à la retraite.**	*zhuh swee zah lah ruh·trayt*

Romance

Would you like to go out for a drink/dinner?	**Voudriez-vous aller prendre un verre/ sortir dîner?** *voo·dreeyay·voo ah·lay prawN·druh uhN vehr/sohr·teer dee·nay*
What are your plans for tonight/ tomorrow?	**Quels sont vos projets pour ce soir/demain?** *kehl sohN voh proh·zhay poor suh swahr/ duh·mehN*
Can I have your (phone) number?	**Puis-je avoir votre numéro (de téléphone)?** *pwee·zhuh ah·vwahr voh·truh new·may·roh (duh tay·lay·fohn)*
Can I join you?	**Puis-je me joindre à vous?** *pwee·zhuh muh zhwehN·druh ah voo*
Can I buy you a drink?	**Puis-je vous offrir un verre?** *pwee·zhuh voo zoh·freer uhN vehr*
I love you.	**Je t'aime.** *zhuh tehm*

Accepting & Rejecting

I'd love to.	**Avec plaisir.** *ah·vehk play·zeer*
Where should we meet?	**Où devons-nous nous retrouver?** *oo duh·vohN·noo noo ruh·troo·vay*
I'll meet you at the bar/your hotel.	**Je vous retrouverai au bar/à votre hôtel.** *zhuh voo ruh·troo·vuh·ray oh bahr/ah voh·truh oh·tehl*
I'll come by at…	**Je viendrai à…** *zhuh veeyehN·dray ah…*
I'm busy.	**Je suis occupé *m*/occupée *f*.** *zhuh swee zoh·kew·pay*
I'm not interested.	**Je ne suis pas intéressé *m*/intéressée *f*.** *zhuh nuh swee pah ehN·tay·reh·say*
Leave me alone.	**Laissez-moi tranquille.** *leh·say mwah trawN·keel*
Stop bothering me!	**Fichez-moi la paix !** *fee·shay·mwah lah pay*

Eating Out

Can you recommend a good restaurant/ bar?	**Pouvez-vous me conseiller un bon restaurant/bar?** *poo·vay·voo muh kohN·say·yay uhN bohN reh·stoh·rawN/bahr*
Is there a traditional French/an inexpensive restaurant nearby?	**Y-a-t-il un restaurant traditionnel français/ bon marché près d'ici?** *yah·teel uhN reh·stoh·rawN trah·dee·seeyohN·nehl frawN·say/ bohN mahr·shay pray dee·see*
A table for..., please.	**Une table pour..., s'il vous plaît.** *ewn tah·bluh poor... seel voo play*
Can we sit...?	**Pouvons-nous nous asseoir...?** *poo·vohN-noo noo zah·swahr...*
here/there	**ici/là** *ee·see/lah*
outside	**dehors** *duh·ohr*
in a non-smoking area	**en zone non-fumeur** *awN zohn nohN-few·muhr*
I'm waiting for someone.	**J'attends quelqu'un.** *zhah·tawN kehl·kuhN*
Where are the toilets?	**Où sont les toilettes?** *oo sohN lay twah·leht*
A menu, please.	**La carte, s'il vous plaît.** *lah kahrt seel voo play*
What do you recommend?	**Que recommandez-vous?** *kuh reh·koh·mawN·day-voo*
I'd like...	**Je voudrais...** *zhuh voo·dray...*
Some more..., please.	**Un peu plus de..., s'il vous plaît.** *uhN puh plew duh... seel voo play*
Enjoy your meal!	**Bon appétit !** *bohN nah·peh·tee*
The check [bill], please.	**L'addition, s'il vous plaît.** *lah·dee·seeyohN seel voo play*

Is service included?	**Est-ce que le service est compris?**
	ehs kuh luh sehr•vees ay kohN•pree
Can I pay by credit card/have a receipt?	**Puis-je payer par carte de crédit/avoir un reçu?**
	pwee•zhuh pay•yay pahr kahrt duh kray•dee/ ah•vwahr uhN ruh•sew

Breakfast

le bacon	bacon
luh beh•kohn	
le pain	bread
luh pehN	
le beurre	butter
luh buhr	
la charcuterie	cold cuts
lah shahr•kew•tuh•ree	
le fromage	cheese
luh froh•mahzh	
l'œuf...	...egg
luhf...	
dur/à la coque	hard-/soft-boiled
dewr/ah lah kohk	
sur le plat	fried
sewr luh plah	

YOU MAY SEE...

COUVERT	cover charge
PRIX FIXE	fixed-price
MENU (DU JOUR)	menu (of the day)
SERVICE (NON) COMPRIS	service (not) included
MENU À LA CARTE	specials

brouillé	scrambled
broo·yay	
la confiture	jam/jelly
lah kohN·fee·tewr	
l'omelette	omelet
lohm·leht	
le pain grillé	toast
luh pehN gree·yay	
la saucisse	sausage
lah soh·sees	
le yaourt	yogurt
luh yah·oort	

Appetizers

kwanga	bread made from cassava
kwan·gah	
la soupe de poisson	soup with small fish,
lah soop duh pwah·sohN	simmered and pureed
la soupe aux légumes/a soupe de tomates	vegetable/tomato soup
lah soop oh lay·gewm/lah soop duh toh·maht	

Yams, cassava, sweet potatoes, okra, rice and other starchy
foods are common in Central African countries alongside meats
such as beef, chicken and goat. **Matoke** (baked plantains) and
ugali (a type of oatmeal made from maize and water) are common in
Rwanda and you will come across variations of these staples in many
different places. Goat is one of the most popular meats.

la soupe de volaille	chicken soup
lah soop duh voh•lie	
salade	salad
sah•lahd	

Meat

le bœuf	beef
luh buhf	
le poulet	chicken
luh poo•lay	
l'agneau	lamb
lah•nyoh	
le porc	pork
luh pohr	
le bifteck	steak
luh beef•tehk	
le veau *luh voh*	veal
le chèvre	goat
luh shay•vruh	

Fish & Seafood

la morue *lah moh•rew*	cod
le hareng *luh ah•rawN*	herring
ndakala *luh oh•mahr*	small dried fish
le saumon *luh soh•mohN*	salmon
la crevette *lah kruh•veht*	shrimp

YOU MAY HEAR...

saignant *say•nyawN*	rare
à point *ah pwehN*	medium
bien cuit *beeyehN kwee*	well-done

Vegetables

les haricots *lay ah•ree•koh*	beans
l'igname *luh eeg•nahm*	yam
la carotte *lah kah•roht*	carrot
lituma *lee•too•mah*	fried mashed plantain balls
le manioc *luh man•ee•yoc*	cassava
le champignon *luh shawN•pee•nyohN*	mushroom
l'oignon *loh•nyohN*	onion
les petits pois *lay puh•tee pwah*	peas
la pomme de terre *lah pohm duh tehr*	potato

| **la tomate** | tomato |
| *lah toh·maht* | |

Sauces & Condiments

sel	salt
sehl	
poivre	pepper
pwah·vruh	
moutarde	mustard
moo·tahrd	
ketchup	ketchup
Ket·shuhp	

Fruit & Dessert

la pomme	apple
lah pohm	
la banane	banana
lah bah·nahn	
le citron	lemon
luh see·trohN	
l'orange	orange
loh·rawNzh	
la poire	pear
lah pwahr	
la fraise	strawberry
lah frehz	
la glace	ice cream
lah glahs	
le chocolat	chocolate
luh shoh·koh·lah	

la vanille *lah vah•neeyuh*	vanilla
la génoise *lah zhay•nwahz*	sponge cake
la tarte aux fruits *lah tahrt oh frwee*	fruit pie or tart
la mousse *lah moos*	chocolate mousse
la crème anglaise *lah krehm awN•glehz*	custard
la crème *lah krehm*	cream

Drinks

Can I see the wine list/ drinks menu, please?	**La carte des vins/boissons, s'il vous plaît.** *lah kahrt day vehN/bwah•sohN seel voo play*
What do you recommend?	**Que me conseillez-vous?** *kuh muh kohN•say•yay•voo*
I'd like a bottle/glass of red/white wine.	**Je voudrais une bouteille/un verre de vin rouge/blanc.** *zhuh voo•dray ewn boo•tehy/uhN vehr duh vehN roozh/blawN*
The house wine, please.	**Le vin de la maison, s'il vous plaît.** *luh vehN duh lah may•zohN seel voo play*
Another bottle/glass, please.	**Une autre bouteille/Un autre verre, s'il vous plaît.** *ewn oh•truh boo•tehy/uhN noh•truh vehr seel voo play*
I'd like a local beer.	**Je voudrais une bière locale.** *zhuh voo•dray ewn beeyehr loh•kahl*
Can I buy you a drink?	**Puis-je vous offrir un verre?** *pwee•zhuh voo zoh•freer uhN vehr*
Cheers!	**Santé !** *sawN•tay*

A coffee/tea, please.	**Un café/thé, s'il vous plaît.**
	uhN kah•fay/tay seel voo play
Black.	**Noir.** *nwahr*
With…	**Avec…** *ah•vehk…*
milk	**du lait** *dew lay*
sugar	**du sucre** *dew sew•kruh*
artificial sweetener	**de l'édulcorant**
	duh lay•dewl•koh•rawN
A…, please.	**Un…, s'il vous plaît.** *uhN… seel voo play*
juice	**jus de fruit** *zhew duh frwee*
soda	**soda** *soh•dah*
sparkling/still water	**de l'eau gazeuse/plate** *duh loh gah•zuhz/plaht*

Beer is a popular alcoholic drink and can provide some welcome refreshment from the heat and humidity. Some different beer brands you may come across include Primus, Mützig and Turbo King, alongside exports such as Amstel and Heineken.

Leisure Time

Sightseeing

Where's the tourist information office?	**Où est l'office de tourisme?** *oo ay loh•fees duh too•ree•smuh*
What are the main sights?	**Quelles sont les choses importantes à voir?** *kehl sohN lay shoh zehN•pohr•tawN tah vwahr*
Do you offer tours in English?	**Proposez-vous des visites en anglais?** *Proh•poh•zay•voo day vee•zeet awN nawN•glay*
Can I have a map/guide?	**Puis-je avoir une carte/un guide?** *pwee•zhuh ah•vwahr ewn kahrt/uhN geed*

> **YOU MAY SEE...**
>
> | | |
> |---|---|
> | **OUVERT/FERMÉ** | open/closed |
> | **ENTRÉE/SORTIE** | entrance/exit |

Shopping

Where's the market/mall?	**Où est le marché/centre commercial?** *oo ay luh mahr·shay/sawN·truh koh·mehr·seeyahl*
I'm just looking.	**Je regarde seulement.** *zhuh ruh·gahrd suhl·mawN*
Can you help me?	**Pouvez-vous m'aider?** *poo·vay·voo meh·day*
I'm being helped.	**On s'occupe de moi.** *ohN soh·kewp duh mwah*
How much?	**Combien ça coûte?** *kohN·beeyehN sah koot*
That one, please.	**Celui-ci *m*/Celle-ci *f*, s'il vous plaît.** *suh·lwee·see/sehl see seel voo play*
I'd like…	**Je voudrais…** *zhuh voo·dray…*
That's all.	**C'est tout.** *say too*
Where can I pay?	**Où puis-je payer?** *oo pwee·zhuh pay·yay*
I'll pay in cash/by credit card.	**Je paierai en espèces/par carte de crédit.** *zhuh pay·ray awN neh·spehs/pahr kahrt duh kray·dee*
A receipt, please.	**Un reçu, s'il vous plaît.** *uhN ruh·sew seel voo play*

Sport & Leisure

When's the game?	**Quand a lieu le match?** *kawN tah leeyuh luh mahtch*
Where's…?	**Où est…?** *oo ay…*
the beach	**la plage** *lah plazh*
the park	**le parc** *luh pahrk*
the pool	**la piscine** *lah pee·seen*
Is it safe to swim here?	**Est-ce que c'est sans danger de nager ici?** *ehs kuh say sawN dawN·zhay duh nah·zhay ee·see*
Can I hire clubs?	**Puis-je louer des clubs?** *pwee·zhuh looway day kluhb*
How much per hour?	**Combien ça coûte par heure?** *kohN·beeyehN sah koot pahr uhr*
How far is it to…?	**À quelle distance se trouve…?** *ah kehl dees·tawNs suh troov…*
Show me on the map, please.	**Montrez-moi sur la carte, s'il vous plaît.** *mohN·tray·mwah sewr lah kahrt seel voo play*

Gabon and Rwanda provide great safari and hiking opportunities with spectacular scenery - think cascading waterfalls and lush rainforest. Travel booked through a reputable tour operator will enhance the experience.

Going Out

What's there to do at night?	**Que peut-on faire le soir?** *kuh puh•tohN fehr luh swahr*
Do you have a program of events?	**Avez-vous un programme des festivités?** *ah•vay•voo uhN proh•grahm day fehs•tee•vee•tay*
What's playing tonight?	**Qui joue ce soir?** *kee zhoo suh swahr*
Where's...?	**Où est...?** *oo ay...*
the downtown area	**le centre ville** *luh sawN•truh veel*
the bar	**le bar** *luh bahr*
the dance club	**la discothèque** *lah dees•koh•tehk*
Is this area safe at night?	**Est-ce que cet endroit est sûr la nuit?** *ehs kuh seht awN•drwah ay sewr lah nwee*

Baby Essentials

Do you have...?	**Avez-vous...?** *ah•vay•voo...*
a baby bottle	**un biberon** *uhN bee•buh•rohN*
baby food	**des petits pots** *day puh•tee poh*
baby wipes	**des lingettes pour bébé** *day lehN•zhet poor bay•bay*
a car seat	**un siège bébé** *uhN seeyehzh bay•bay*
a children's menu/portion	**un menu/des portions pour enfants** *uhN muh•new/day pohr•seeyohN poo rawN•fawN*

a child's seat/	**un siège bébé/une chaise haute**
highchair	*uhN seeyehzh bay·bay/ewn shehz oht*
a crib/cot	**un berceau/lit pliant** *uhN behr·soh/lee pleeyawN*
diapers [nappies]	**des couches** *day koosh*
formula	**du lait pour bébé** *dew lay poor bay·bay*
a pacifier [dummy]	**une tétine** *ewn tay·teen*
a playpen	**un parc pour enfant** *uhN pahrk poo rawN·fawN*
a stroller	**une poussette** *ewn poo·seht*
[pushchair]	
Can I breastfeed	**Puis-je allaiter le bébé ici?**
the baby here?	*pwee·zhuh ah·leh·tay luh bay·bay ee·see*
Where can I	**Où puis-je allaiter/changer le bébé?**
breastfeed/change	*oo pwee·zhuh ah·leh·tay/shawN·zhay luh bay·bay*
the baby?	

For Eating Out, see page 167.

Disabled Travelers

Is there...?	**Y-a-t-il...?** *yah·teel...*
access for	**un accès pour handicapés**
the disabled	*uhN nahk·seh poor awN·dee·kah·pay*
a wheelchair ramp	**un accès pour chaises roulantes**
	uhN nahk·say poor shehz roo·lawNt
a disabled-	**des toilettes accessibles aux handicapés**
accessible toilet	*day twah·leht ahk·seh·see·bluh oh zawN·dee·kah·pay*
I need...	**J'ai besoin...** *zhay buh·zwehN...*
assistance	**d'aide** *dehd*
an elevator [a lift]	**d'un ascenseur** *duhN nah·sawN·suhr*
a ground-floor	**d'une chambre au rez-de-chaussée**
room	*dewn shawN·bruh oh ray·duh·shoh·say*
Please speak louder.	**S'il vous plaît, parlez plus fort.**
	seel voo play pahr·lay plew fohr

Health & Emergencies

Emergencies

Help!	**Au secours!** *oh suh•koor*
Go away!	**Allez-vous en!** *ah•lay•voo zawN*
Stop, thief!	**Arrêtez, au voleur!** *ah•reh•tay oh voh•luhr*
Get a doctor!	**Allez chercher un docteur!**
	ah•lay shehr•shay uhN dohk•tuhr
Fire!	**Au feu!** *oh fuh*

YOU MAY HEAR...

Remplissez ce formulaire.	Fill out this form.
rawN•plee•say suh fohr•mew•lehr	
Vos papiers d'identité, s'il vous plaît.	Your ID, please.
voh pah•peeyay dee•dawN•tee•tay seel voo play	
Quand/Où cela s'est-il produit?	When/Where did
kawN/oo suh•lah say•teel proh•dwee	it happen?
À quoi ressemble-t-il *m*/ressemble-t-elle *f*?	What does he/she
ah kwah ruh•sawN•bluh•teel/ruh•sawN•bluh•tehl	look like?

Check the local emergency numbers upon arrival or in advance of travel and keep them to hand. These will vary depending on your destination.

I'm lost.	**Je suis perdu** *m*/**perdue** *f*. *zhuh swee pehr·dew*
Can you help me?	**Pouvez-vous m'aider?** *poo·vay·voo may·day*
Call the police!	**Appelez la police!** *ah·puh·lay lah poh·lees*
Where's the police station?	**Où est le commissariat de police?** *oo ay luh koh·mee·sah·reeyah duh poh·lees*
My child is missing.	**Mon enfant a disparu.** *mohN nawN·fawN ah dees·pah·rew*

Health

I'm sick.	**Je suis malade.** *zhuh swee mah·lahd*
I need an English-speaking doctor.	**J'ai besoin d'un docteur qui parle anglais.** *zhay buh·zwehN duhN dohk·tuhr kee pahrl awN·glay*
It hurts here.	**Ça fait mal ici.** *sah fay mahl ee·see*
Where's the pharmacy?	**Où est la pharmacie?** *oo ay lah fahr·mah·see*
I'm (...months) pregnant.	**Je suis enceinte (de...mois).** *zhuh swee zawN·sehNt (duh...mwah)*
I'm on...	**Je prends...** *zhuh prawN...*
I'm allergic to antibiotics/penicillin.	**Je suis allergique aux antibiotiques/ à la pénicilline.** *zhuh swee zah·lehr·zheek oh zawN·tee·beeyoh·teek/ah lah pay·nee·see·leen*

a un *m*/une *f*
acetaminophen le paracétamol
adapter l'adaptateur
and et
antiseptic cream la crème antiseptique
aspirin l'aspirine
baby le bébé
backpack le sac à dos
bad mauvais(e)
bag le sac
bandage le pansement
battleground le champ de bataille
beige beige
bikini le bikini
bird l'oiseau
black noir
bland sans goût
blue bleu
bottle opener l'ouvre-bouteille
bowl le saladier
boy le garçon
boyfriend le petit-ami
bra le soutien-gorge
brown marron
camera l'appareil photo;
can opener le l'ouvre-boîte
castle le château
charger charger

cigarette la cigarette
cold (sickness) le rhume;
  ~ **(temperature)** froid
comb le peigne
computer l'ordinateur
condom le préservatif
contact lens solution la solution pour lentilles de contact
corkscrew le tire-bouchon
cup la tasse
dangerous dangereux
deodorant le déodorant
diabetic diabétique
doll la poupée
fly la mouche
fork la fourchette
girl la fille
girlfriend la petite-amie
glass le verre;
good adj bon
gray gris
green vert
hairbrush la brosse
hairspray la laque
hot (spicy) épicé;
  ~ **(temperature)** chaud;
husband le mari
ice la glace
icy glacé

injection la piqûre
I'd like… Je voudrais…
insect repellent la lotion anti-insectes
jeans le jean
knife le couteau
lactose intolerant allergique au lactose
large grand
lighter le briquet
lotion la crème
love v (**someone**) aimer; ~ n amour
matches d'allumettes
medium (size) moyen
museum le musée
nail file la lime á ongle
napkin la serviette
nurse l'infirmier
orange (color) orange
park v se garer; ~ n le parc
pen le stylo
plate l'assiette
purple pourpre
pajamas un pyjama
rain la pluie
raincoat l'imperméable
razor blade la lame de rasoir
razor, disposable un rasoir (jetable)
red rouge
salty salé
sandals les sandales

sanitary napkin la serviette hygiénique
scissors les ciseaux
shampoo/conditioner du shampooing/de l'après shampooing
shoes les chaussures
small petit(e)
snake le serpent
sneakers les tennis
snowy neigeux
soap le savon
sock la chaussette
spicy épicé
spider l'araignée (f)
spoon la cuillère
stamp n (**postage**) le timbre
suitcase la valise
sun le soleil
sunblock l'écran solaire
sunglasses les lunettes de soleil
sweater le pull
sweatshirt le sweat-shirt
swimsuit le maillot de bain
tampon le tampon
terrible terrible
tie (clothing) la cravate
tissues les Kleenex
toilet paper le papier toilette
toothbrush la brosse
toothpaste le dentifrice

tough (food) dur
toy le jouet
underwear les sous-vêtements
vegan végétalien *m*/végétalienne *f*
vegetarian végétarien
white blanc
wife l'épouse
with avec
without sans
yellow jaune
your votre
zoo le zoo

Swahili

Essentials

Hello/Hi.	**Helo/Hujambo.**	*Helo/Hoo·jam·boh*
Goodbye.	**Kwa heri.**	*Kwah heh·ree*
Yes/No/Okay.	**Ndiyo/Hapana/Sawa.**	*Ndi·yoh/Hah·pah·nah/ Sah·wah*
Excuse me! (to get attention)	**Samahani!**	*Sah·mah·hah·nee!*
Excuse me. (to get past)	**Tafadhali!**	*Tah·fah·thah·lee*
I'm sorry.	**Samahani.**	*Sah·mah·hah·nee*
I'd like...	**Ningependa...**	*Neen·geh·pen·dah...*
How much?	**N·gah·pee?**	*N·ga·pi?*
And/or.	**Na/au.**	*Nah/ah·oo*
Please.	**Tafadhali.**	*Tah·fah·thah·lee*
Thank you.	**Asante.**	*Ah·sah·nteh*
You're welcome.	**Umekaribishwa**	*Oo·meh·kah·ree·bee·sh·wah*
Where's...?	**...ni wapi...?**	*...nee·wah·pee...?*
I'm going to...	**Naenda...**	*Nah·en·dah...*
My name is...	**Jina langu ni...**	*Jee·nah lah·n·goo nee...*
Please speak slowly.	**Tafadhali zungumza pole pole.**	*Tah·fah·thah·lee zoon·goom·zah poh·leh poh·leh*
Can you repeat that?	**Tafadhali rudia?**	*Tah·fah·thah·lee roo·dee·ah*
I don't understand.	**Sielewi.**	*See·eh·leh·wee*
Do you speak English?	**Unaweza kuzungumza Kingereza?**	*Oo·nah·weh·zah koo·zoon·goo·m·zah Keen·geh·reh·zah?*
I don't speak (much) Swahili.	**Sizungumzi (mengi) Swahili.**	*See·zoon·goo·m·zee (men·gee) Swahili*
Where's the restroom [toilet]?	**Vyoo viko wapi [toilet]?**	*V·yoo vee·koh wah·pee?*
Help!	**Saidia!**	*Nee·sah·ee·dee·eh!*

You'll find the pronunciation of the Swahili letters and words written in gray after each sentence to guide you. Simply pronounce these as if they were English, noting that stress is always on the next to last syllable. Swahili is relatively easy to pronounce and as you hear the language being spoken, you will quickly become accustomed to the local pronunciation and dialect.

Numbers

0	**sufuri** *soo·foo·ree*
1	**moja** *moh·jah*
2	**mbili** *mbee·lee*
3	**tatu** *tah·too*
4	**nne** *n·neh*
5	**tano** *tah·noh*
6	**sita** *see·tah*
7	**saba** *sah·bah*
8	**nane** *nah·neh*
9	**tisa** *tee·sah*
10	**kumi** *koo·mee*
11	**kumi na moja** *koo·mee nah moh·jah*
12	**kumi na mbili** *koo·mee na mbee·lee*
13	**kumi na tatu** *koo·mee nah tah·tuh*
14	**kumi na nne** *koo·mee nah n·neh*
15	**kumi na tano** *koo·mee nah tah·noh*
16	**kumi na sita** *koo·mee nah see·tah*
17	**kumi na saba** *koo·mee nah sah·bah*
18	**kumi na nane** *koo·mee nah nah·neh*
19	**kumi na tisa** *koo·mee nah tee·sah*
20	**ishirini** *eesh·ee·ree·nee*

21	**ishirini na moja** eesh·ee·ree·nee nah moh·jah
30	**thelathinini** theh·lah·thee·nee
50	**hamsini** ham·see·nee
60	**sitini** see·tee·nee
70	**sabini** sah·bee·nee
80	**themanini** theh·mah·nee·nee
90	**tisini** tee·see·nee
100	**mia moja** mee·ah moh·jah
101	**mia moja na moja** mee·ah moh·jah nah moh·jah
200	**mia mbili** mee·ah mbee·lee
500	**mia tano** mee·ah tah·noh
1,000	**elfu moja** el·foo moh·jah
10,000	**elfu kumi** el·foo koo·mee
1,000,000	**milioni moja** mee·lee·oh·nee moh·jah

Time

What time is it?	**Ni saa ngapi?** Nee saah n·gah·pee
It's midday.	**Ni mchana.** Nee m·chah·nah
Five past three.	**Ni saa tisa na dakika tano.** Nee saah tee·sah nah dah·kee·kah tah·noh
A quarter to ten.	**Saa nne kasorobo.** Saah n·neh kah·soh·roh·boh
5:30 a.m./p.m.	**11:30 asubuhi/jioni** Ah·soo·boo·hee/jee·oh·nee

Swahili is a Bantu language spoken primarily in Kenya, Tanzania and Uganda. There are several dialects of Swahili but in this book we have used standard Swahili.

Days

Monday	**Jumatatu** *Joo-mah-tah-too*
Tuesday	**Jumanne** *Joo-mah-n-neh*
Wednesday	**Jumatano** *Joo-mah-tah-noh*
Thursday	**Alhamisi** *Al-hah-mee-see*
Friday	**Ijumaa** *Ee-joo-maah*
Saturday	**Jumamosi** *Joo-ma-mo-see*
Sunday	**Jumapili** *Joo-ma-pee-lee*

Dates

yesterday	**jana** *jah-nah*
today	**Leo** *Leh-oh*
tomorrow	**Kesho** *Keh-shoh*
day	**Siku** *See-koo*
week	**Juma/wiki** *Joo-mah/wee-kee*
month	**Mwezi** *M-weh-zee*
year	**Mwaka** *M-wah-kah*
Happy New Year!	**Furahia siku kuu ya mwaka mpya!** *Foo-rah-hee-ah see-koo koo yah m-wah-kah m-p-yah!*
Happy Birthday!	**Furahia siku ya kuzaliwa!** *Foo-rah-hee-ah see-koo yah koo-zah-lee-wah!*

Months

January	**Januari** *Jah-noo-ah-ree*
February	**Februari** *Feb-roo-ah-ree*
March	**Machi** *Mah-chee*
April	**Aprili** *A-pree-lee*
May	**mei** *meh-ee*
June	**Juni** *Joo-nee*
July	**Julai** *Joo-lah-ee*
August	**Agosti** *Ah-goh-stee*

September	**Septemba** Sep·teh·m·bah
October	**Oktoba** Oh·kto·bah
November	**Novemba** Noh·veh·m·bah
December	**Disemba** Dee·seh·m·bah

Arrival & Departure

I'm on vacation [holiday]/business.	**Niko mapumzikoni (holidei)/biashara.** Nee·koh mah·poo·m·zee·koh·nee(see·koo koo)/bia·sha· ra
I'm going to...	**Naenda...** Nah·eh·n·dah ...
I'm staying at the...Hotel.	**Naishi ... Hoteli.** Nah·ee·shee ...Hoh·teh·lee

Many bus companies and tour operators run swift and economic inter-city buses and express saloon car services. **Local buses** are cheap and the easiest way to get to most places but will not depart until overcrowded. **Matatus** are privately-owned, adapted minivans which usually travel at terrifying speeds with more expensive fares than the local buses.

Money

Where's...?	**...iko wapi?** ... ee·koh wah·pee?
the ATM	**ATM**
the bank	**benki** ben·kee
the currency exchange office	**afisi ya ubadilishanaji wa pesa** ah·fee·see yah oo· bah·dee·lee·shah·nah·jee wah peh·sah
When does the bank open/close?	**Benki hufunguliwa/hufungwa saa ngapi?** Ben·kee hoo·foo·ngoo·lee·wah/hoo·foo·n·gwah saah n·gah·pee?

I'd like to change dollars/pounds sterling/euros into shillings.	**Ningependa kubadilisha dola/pauni/yuro Hadi Shilingi.** *Neen•geh•pen•dah koo•bah•dee•lee•shah doh•lah/pah•oo•nee/yoo•roh hah•dee shee•leen•gee.*
I'd like to cash traveler's cheques.	**Ningependa kupeana cheki ya usafiri.** *Nee•n•geh• peh•n•dah ku•peh•ah•nah cheh•kee yah oo•sah•fee•ree*
Can I pay in cash?	**Naweza kulipa kwa pesa taslimu?** *Nah•weh•zah koo•lee•pah kwah peh•sah tas•lee•moo?*
Can I pay by (credit) card?	**Ninaweza kulipia kwa kadi (ya mkopo)?** *Nah•weh• zah koo•lee•pae kwah kah•dee (yah m•koh•poh)?*

For Numbers, see page 188.

YOU MAY SEE…

Uganda, Kenya and Tanzania each have their own currency – **Ugandan, Kenyan and Tanzanian Shillings** respectively. Note that it is not possible to exchange or use Kenyan Shillings in Tanzania, and vice versa.

Getting Around

How do I get to town?	**Njia ya kwenda mjini?** *N•jee•ah yah k•wen•dah m•jee•nee nee ganee?*
Where's…?	**… iko wapi?** *……ee•koh wah•pee?*
the airport	**Uwanja wa ndege** *oo•wan•jah wah n•deh•geh*
the train station	**Stesheni ya gari la moshi** *ste•she•nee• ya ga•ree• la•mo•shee*
the bus station	**Stesheni ya basi** *steh•sheh•nee• yah yah bah•see*
Is it far from here?	**Ni mbali kutoka hapa?** *Nee m•bah•lee koo•toh•kah hah•pah?*
Where do I buy a ticket?	**Nitanunua wapi tiketi?** *Nee•tah•noo•noo•ah• wah•pee• tee•keh•tee*
A one-way/return-trip ticket to…	**Ya kwenda/ya kwenda na kurudi…** *Ya• kwen•dah/yah kwen•dah nah koo•roo•dee…*
How much?	**Ni ngapi?** *Nee n•gah•pee?*
Which gate/line?	**Ni mlango upi/laini ipi?** *Nee m•lahn•goh oo•pee/lah•ee•nee ee•pee?*
Which platform?	**Jukwaa lipi?** *Joo•kwaa lee•pee?*
Where can I get a taxi?	**Naweza kupata wapi teksi?** *Nah•weh•zah kuh•pah•tah wah•pih tek•see?*
Take me to this address.	**Nielekeze kwenye sehemu hii.** *Nee•eh•leh•keh•zeh hah•pah*
To…Airport, please.	**… uwanja wa ndege, Tafadhali.** *… oo•wan•jah wah n•deh•geh, Tah•fah•thah•lee*
I'm in a rush.	**Nina haraka.** *Nee•nah hah•rah•kah*
Can I have a map?	**Naweza kupata ramani?** *Nah•weh•zah koo•pah•tah rah•mah•nee?*

I don't speak (much) Shona.	**Handinyatsogone Shona.** ha·ndi·nya·tso·go·ne Sho·na
Where's the restroom [toilet]?	**Chimbuzi ndochiwana kupi?** chee·mboo·zee ndoh·chee·wa·ne·pee
Help!	**Ndibatsireiwo!** ndi·ba·tsi·reh·o

You'll find the pronunciation of the Shona letters and words written in gray after each sentence to guide you. Simply pronounce these as if they were English; as you hear the language being spoken, you will quickly become accustomed to the local pronunciation and dialect.

Numbers

0	zero	ze·ro
1	hwani	hwa·ni
2	tuu	too
3	thrii	the·ree
4	fuo	fo·o
5	faifi	far·yeeh
6	sikisi	see·kee·si
7	sevheni	si·v·
8	eyiti	eh·yee·
9	naini	na·yee·
10	teni	teh·ni
11	ilevheni	ee·le·
12	twerufu	too·

13	**theyitini** *thur·yee·tee·ni*
14	**footini** *fo·o·tee·ni*
15	**fifitini** *fi·fi·tee·ni*
16	**sikisitini** *see·kee·si·tee·ni*
17	**sevhenitini** *sir·ve·nee·tee·ni*
18	**eyitini** *ir·yee·tee·ni*
19	**nainitini** *nah·yee·nee·tee·ni*
20	**twendi** *too·we·nti*
21	**twendi·hwani** *twe·nti·hwa·ni*
30	**theti** *ther·ti*
40	**foti** *fo·ti*
50	**fifiti** *fi·fi·ti*
60	**sikisiti** *see·kee·si·ti*
70	**sevheniti** *sir·ve·nee·ti*
80	**eyiti** *ir·yee·tee*
90	**nainiti** *nu·yee·nee·ti*
100	**hwani handuredhi** *hwa·ni han·doo·re*
101	**hwani hand**
200	**tuu h**
500	**faifi**
1,000	**hwa**
10,000	**t**
1,000,000	

How much…?	**Ni pesa ngapi…?** *Nee peh·sah n·gah·pee*
per day/week	**kwa siku/wiki** *k·wah see·koo/wee·kee*
Are there any discounts?	**Kuna diskaunti zozote?** *Koo·nah dees·kah·oo·n·tee zoh·zoh·teh*

Places to Stay

Can you recommend a hotel?	**Tafadhali nipendekezee hoteli?** *Tah·fah·thah·lee nee·peh·n·deh·ke·z·eeh hoh·teh·lee*
I made a re...... ...ifadhia. *Nee·meh·koo·hee·fah·thee·ah*	
My n...	Jee·nah lah·n·goo nee …
Do...	·nah choo·mbah
	chah m·too m·moh·jah/
	h nah bah·foo
	h·ooh nah
	h
	oh·jah

How much?	**Ni pesa ngapi?** *Nee peh·sah n·gah·pee*
Is there anything cheaper?	**Je, kuna chochote cha bei rahisi?** *Jeh, koo·nah choh·choh·teh chah beh·ee rah·hee·see*
When's checkout?	**Kuondoka ni lini?** *Koo·oh·n·doh·kah nee lee·nee?*
Can I leave this in the safe?	**Naweza kuwacha hii kwenye kisanduku imara?** *Nah·weh·zah koo·wah·chah hee kweh·n·yeh kee·sah·n·doo·koo ee·mah·rah*
Can I leave my bags?	**naweza kuwacha mifuko yangu?** *Nah·weh·zah koo·wah·chah mee·foo·koh yah·n·goo?*
Can I have my bill/ a receipt?	**naweza kupata bili/risiti yangu?** *Nah·weh·zah koo·pah·tah bee·lee/ree·see·tee yah·n·goo?*
I'll pay in cash/ by credit card.	**nitalipa kwa pesa taslimu/kadi ya mkopo.** *Nee·tah·lee·pah kwah peh·sah tah·s·lee·moo/ kah·dee yah m·koh·poh*

There is a wide variety of accomodations available from safari lodges and tented camps to roadside motels, African **banda** (thatched huts), and furnished beachside bungalows. For longer stays, guest houses are a good bet.

Money

Where's…?	**Ndekupi kune…?** ndeh-coo-pi coo-ne…
the ATM	**mushina wekutorera mari/ATM** moo-shee-nah weh coo-to-rah mah-ree/ATM
the bank	**bhengi** beh-ngi
the currency exchange office	**bheruu dhichaji** beh-roo dee-char-ji
When does the bank open/close?	**Bhengi rinovhura/rinovhara nguvai?** be-ngi ree-no-voo-ra/ree-no-va-ra ngu-va-yee
I'd like to change dollars/pounds sterling/euros into…	**Ndiri kuda kuchinja madhora/mapaunzi/mayuro kuenda ku…** ndi-ri coo-da coo-chee-nja mah-door-ra/mah-pah-woo-nzi/mah-yu-ro coo-ye-nda coo…
I'd like to cash traveler's cheques.	**Ndiri kuda kuchinja maturavhera cheki.** ndi-ree coo-da coo-chee-nja mah-too-ra-ve-ra che-ki
Can I pay in cash?	**Ndinokwanisa kubhadhara iri mari here?** ndi-no-kua-nee-sa coo-bah-dar-ra ee-ree mah-ree heh-reh
Can I pay by (credit) card?	**Ndinokwanisa kubhadhara nekadhi here?** ndi-no-kua-nee-sa coo-bah-dar-ra ne-car-di heh-reh

For Numbers, see page 82.

For Numbers, see page 82.

YOU MAY SEE…

In Zimbabwe you can pay in US dollars, South African rand, Botswana pula and even British pounds sterling.

Getting Around

How do I get to town?	**Ndingasvike sei kutaundi?** *ndi·nga·svi·ke sir·yee coo·tah·woo·ndi?*
Where's . . .?	**Ndekupi kune . . .?** *nde·coo·pi coo·ne. . .?*
the airport	**Eyapoti** *eh·ya·poh·ti*
the train station	**Chiteshi chechitima** *chee·teh·shi che·chee·tee·ma*
the bus station	**Chiteshi chebhazi** *chee·teh·shi che·bah·zee*
Is it far from here?	**Kure here nepano?** *coo·reh heh·reh neh·pah·no*
Where do I buy a ticket?	**Ndinotenga kupi tiketi?** *ndi·no·te·nga coo·pi tee·ke·ti*
A one-way/return-trip ticket to. . .	**Ndinoda tiketi rekuenda ku. . .** *ndi·no·da tee·ke·ti reh·coo·ye·nda coo. . .*
How much?	**Imarii?** *ee·mah·ree*
Which gate/line?	**Ndoshandisa gedhi ripi?** *ndo·shah·ndi·sa ge·di ree·pi?*
Which platform?	**Ndokwirira papi?** *ndo·kwi·ree·ra pa·pi*
Where can I get a taxi?	**Ndekupi kwandingawana tekisi?** *nde·coo·pi kua·ndi·nga·wa·na teh·kee·si?*
Take me to this address.	**Ndiendesewo panzvimbo iyi.** *ndi·ye·nde·se·o pah·nzvi·mbo ee·yee*

Social Media

Are you on Facebook/Twitter?	**Je uko kwenye Facebook/Tweeter?** *Jeh oo·ko kwen·yeh Facebook/Tweeter?*
What's your username?	**Jina lako la mtumiaji ni lipi?** *Jee·nah lah·koh lah m·too·mee·ah·jee nee lee·pee?*
I'll add you as a friend.	**Nitakuongeza kama rafiki yangu.** *Nee·tah·koo·ooh·n·geh·zah kah·mah rah·fee·kee yan·goo*
I'll follow you on Twitter.	**Nitakufuatilia kwenye Twittter.** *Nee·tah·koo·foo·ah·tee·lee·ah kwen·yeh Tweeter*
Are you following…?	**Je unafuata…?** *Jeh oo·nah·foo·ah·tah…?*
I'll put the pictures on Facebook/Twitter.	**Nitaziweka picha kwenye Facebook/Tweeter.** *Nee·tah·zee·weh·kah pee·chah kwen·yeh Facebook/tweeter*
I'll tag you in the pictures.	**Nitakutaja kwenye picha.** *Nee·tah·koo·tah·jah kwen·yeh pee·chah*

Conversation

Hello!/Hi!	**Helo! /Jambo!** *Heh·loh! /Jam·boh!*
How are you?	**Habari yako?** *Hah·bah·ree yah·koh?*
Fine, thanks.	**Njema, nashukuru.** *N·jeh·mah, nah·shoo·koo·roo.*
Excuse me!	**Samahani!** *Sah·mah·hah·nee!*
Do you speak English?	**Je unazungumza Kiingereza?** *Jeh, oo·nah·zoon·goo·m·zah Keen·geh·reh·zah?*
What's your name?	**Unaitwa nani?** *Oo·nah·ee·t·wah nah·nee?*
My name is…	**Jina langu ni…** *Jee·nah lah·n·goo nee…*
Nice to meet you.	**Nashukuru kukutana nawe.** *Nah·sh·oo·koo·roo koo·koo·tah·nah nah·weh*
Where are you from?	**Unatoka wapi?** *Oo·nah·toh·kah wah·pee?*
I'm from the U.K./U.S.	**Natoka Uingereza/Marekani** *Nah·toh·kah Uoo·ee·n·geh·reh·zah/mah·reh·kah·nee*

What do you do for a living?	**Wewe unafanya kazi gani?** *Weh·weh oo·nah·fah·n·yah kah·zee gah·nee?*
I work for…	**Nafanyia kazi…** *Nah·fah·n·yee·ah kah·zee…*
I'm a student.	**Mimi ni mwanafunzi.** *Mee·mee nee m·wah·nah·foo·n·zee*
I'm retired.	**Nimestaafu.** *Nee·meh·stah·ah·foo*

Romance

Would you like to go out for a drink/dinner?	**Ungependa twende tukapate kinywaji/chakula cha jioni?** *Oo·n·geh·peh·n·dah t·weh·n·deh too·kah·pah·teh kee·n·y·wah·jee/ch·ah·koo·lah ch·ah jee·ooh·nee?*
What are your plans for tonight/tomorrow?	**Unapanga kufanya nini leo usiku/kesho?** *Oo·nah·pah·n·gah koo·fan·yah nee·nee leh·ooh oo·see·koo/keh·shoh*
Can I have your (phone) number?	**Tafadhali nipe nambari yako ya (simu).** *Tah·fah·thah·lee nee·peh nam·bah·ree yah·koh (yah see·moo)*
Can I join you?	**Naweza kujiunga nawe?** *Nah·weh·zah koo·jee·oo·n·gah nah·weh?*

How much...?	**I marii...?** *ee-mah-ree...?*
per day/week	**pazuva/pavhiki** *pah-zoo-va/pah-vee-ki*
Are there any	**Mune madhisikaundi here?**
discounts?	*moo-ne mah-di-si-car-woo-ndi heh-reh?*

YOU MAY HEAR...

mberi kwatakananga *mbe-ree kua-ta-car-na-nga*	straight ahead
kuruboshwe *coo-roo-bo-shwe*	left
kurudyi *coo-roo-dyi*	right
patinokona *pah-tee-no-ko-na*	around the corner
pakatarisana ne... *pah-car-ta-ree-sa-na neh...*	opposite
pamashure pe... *pah-mah-shoo-reh peh...*	behind
pamberi pe... *pah-mbe-ree peh...*	next to
tapfuura *tah-pfoo-woo-ra*	after
chamhembe/maodzanyemba *cha-mhe-mbe/mah-o-dza-nye-mba*	north/south
mabvazuva/madokero *mah-bva-zoo-va/mah-do-ke-ro*	east/west
parobhoti *pah-ro-bo-ti*	at the traffic light
panosangana migwagwa *pah-no-sa-nga-na mee-gua-gua*	at the intersection

Can you recommend a hotel?	**Ndingaende kuhotera ipi?**	ndi·nga·ye·nde coo·ho·te·ra ee·pi?
I made a reservation.	**Ndakabhuka**	nda·car·boo·car
My name is. . .	**Ndinonzi. . .**	ndi·no·nzi
Do you have a room...?	**Pane rumu... here?**	pah·ne roo·moo... heh·reh?
for one/two	**yemumwechete/yevaviri**	ye·moo·mwe·che·te/ ye·va·vi·ree
with a bathroom	**ine bhathirumu**	ee·ne bah·the·roo·moo
with air conditioning	**ine eyakondisheni**	ee·ne ch·yah·ko·ndi·share·ni
For...	**Kwe... kue...**	
tonight	**usiku humwechete**	oo·si·e·coo who·mwe·che·te
two nights	**usiku huviri**	oo·see·coo whoo·vi·ree
one week	**vhiki**	vee·ki
How much?	**Imarii?**	ee·mah·ree
Is there anything cheaper?	**Pane yakati chipei here?**	pah·ne ya·car·chee·pah heh·reh?
When's checkout?	**Tinofanirwa kubuda nguvai?**	tee·no·fa·nee·rwa coo·bu·da ngu·va·yee
Can I leave this in the safe?	**Ndinokwanisa kuisa izvi musefa here?**	ndi·no·kua·nee·sa coo·yee·sa ee·zvi moo·sir·fa heh·reh?
Can I leave my bags?	**Ndinokwanisa kusiya mabhegi angu here?**	ndi·no·kua·nee·sa coo·see·ya mah·beh·gee ah·ngu heh·reh?
Can I have my bill/ a receipt?	**Ndingawanawo bhiri/risiti here?**	ndi·nga·wa·na·o bee·ree/ree·see·ti heh·reh?
I'll pay in cash/ by credit card.	**Ndichabhadhara nemari/nekadhi.**	ndi·cha·bah·dah·ra ne·mah·ree/ne·car·di

Is service included?	**Huduma imejumuishwa?** *hoo·doo·mah ee·meh·joo·moo·ee·sh·wah*
Can I pay by credit card/have a receipt?	**Naweza kulipa kwa kadi ya mkopo/kupata risiti?** *Nah·weh·zah koo·lee·pah k·wah kah·dee ya m·koh·poh/koo·pah·tah ree·see·tee?*

YOU MAY SEE...

MALIPO YA BIMA	cover charge
BEI ISIYOBADILIKA	fixed price
MENYU (YA SIKU)	menu (of the day)
HUDUMA IMEJUMUISHWA/	service included/
HAIJAJUMUISHWA	service not included
VYAKULA MAALUM	specials

Breakfast

bacon	**bekoni**
	beh•koh•nee
bread	**mkate**
	m•kah•teh
butter	**siagi**
	see•ah•gee
cold cuts	**vipande baridi vya nyama**
	vee•pan•deh bah•ree•dee v•yah ŋah•mah
cheese	**jibini**
	jee•bee•nee
...egg	**yai**
	yah•ee
hard/soft boiled	**ngumu/laini chemsha**
	n•goo•moo/lah•ee•nee cheh•m•shah
fried	**kaanga**
	kah•an•gah
scrambled	**bumburusha**
	boom•boo•roo•shah
jam/jelly	**jemu/mafuta**
	jeh•moo/mah•foo•tah
omelet	**omleti**
	oh•m•leh•tee
toast	**tosti**
	toh•s•tee
sausage	**soseji**
	soh•seh•jee
yogurt	**gururu**
	goo•roo•roo

The Shona are farming people, also known for their excellent craftmanship, pottery and sculpture. Traditional villages are generally run by patrilineal leaders and traditionally consisted of mud and wattle huts, **rondavels** (round-shaped huts) and livestock **kraals**. Magic and witchcraft remain important methods of social control and are often used as a means to explain various occurences and disasters.

Social Media

Are you on Facebook/ Twitter?	**Muri paFesibhuku/Twita here?** *moo-ri pah-...*
What's your username?	**Yuzanemu yenyu ndeipi?** *you-za-ne-moo ye-...*
I'll add you as a friend.	**Ndichaita kuti muve shamwari yangu.** *ndi-...ve-ra moo-ti moo-ve shah-mwaa-ri ya-ngu*
I'll follow you on Twitter.	**Ndichamutevera paTwita.** *...cha-moo-te-ve-ra pah-Twi-tah*
Are you following...?	**Muri kutevera... here?** *...koo-teh-ve-ra...heh-reh*
I'll put the pictures on Facebook/Twitter.	**Ndichaisa mifananidzo yacho paFesibhuku/ Twita.** *...cha-yee-sa mee-fa-na-nee-dzo ...pah-Fesi-boo-coo/Twi-tah*
I'll tag you in the pictures.	**Ndichakutegai pamifananidzo yacho.** *...nch-mee-fa-na-nee-dzo ya-cho*

Conversation

Hello!/Hi!	**Mhoroi!/Ndeipi?**	*mo-roy/n-day-pi*
How are you?	**Makadii?**	*ma-ka-dee*
Fine, thanks.	**Zvakanaka, ndatenda.**	*zva-ka-na-ka, n-da-ten-da*
Excuse me!	**Pamusoroi!**	*pa-mu-so-roy*
Do you speak English?	**Munotaura Chirungu here?**	*mu-no-ta-u-ra chi-run-gu he-re*
What's your name?	**Manonzi ani?**	*ma-non-zi a-ni*
My name is...	**Ndinonzi ...**	*n-di-non-zi*
Pleased to meet you.	**Ndafara kusangana nemi.**	*n-da-fa-ra ku-san-ga-na ne-mi*
Where are you from?	**Munobva kupi?**	*mu-no-bva ku-pi*
I'm from the U.K./U.S.	**Ndinobva kuUK/kuAmerica.**	*n-di-no-bva ku-u-ka/ku-a-me-ri-ca*
What do you do for a living?	**Munoitei muupenyu?**	*mu-no-i-tey mu-u-pe-nyu*
I work for...	**Ndinoshanda ku...**	*n-di-no-shan-da ku...*
I'm a student.	**Ndiri mudzidzi**	*n-di-ri mu-dzi-dzi*
I'm retired.	**Ndakazorora zvekushanda.**	*n-da-ka-zo-ro-ra zve-ku-shan-da*

Vegetables

Beans	**Maharagwe**
	mah·hah·rah·g·weh
Cabbage	**Kabeji**
	kah·beh·jee
Carrots	**Karoti**
	kah·roh·tee
Mushroom	**Uyoga**
	oo·yoh·gah
Onion	**Kitunguu**
	kee·too·n·goo·uoo
Peas	**Mbaazi**
	m·bah·ah·zee
Potato	**Viazi**
	vee·ah·zee
Tomato	**Nyanya**
	ɲah·ɲah

Sauces & Condiments

Salt	**Chumvi**
	choo·m·vee
Pepper	**Pilipili**
	pee·lee·pee·lee

Due to its Indian influence, East Africa is renowned for its curry specialities. Try **mchuzi wa kuku** (chicken curry prepared with carrots, onions and tomatoes).

Mustard	**Haradali**
	hah•rah•dah•lee
Ketchup	**Achali rojo**
	Ah•chah•lee roh•joh

Fruit & Dessert

Apple	**Tufaha**
	too•fah•hah
Banana	**Ndizi**
	n•dee•zee
Lemon	**Ndimu**
	n•dee•moo
Orange	**Chungwa**
	choo•n•gwah
Pear	**Pea**
	peh•ah
Strawberries	**Stroberi**
	stroh•beh•ree
ice cream	**aiskrimu**
	ah•ees•kree•moo

chocolate/vanilla	**chokoleti/vanila** *choh·koh·leh·tee/vah·nee·lah*
tart/cake	**keki** *keh·kee*
mousse	**mosi** *moh·see*
custard/cream	**mtindi/krimu** *m·teen·dee/kree·moo*

Drinks

The wine list/drink menu, please.	**Tafadhali nipe orodha ya mvinyo/orodha ya vinywaji.** *tah·fah·thah·lee nee·peh ooh·roh·thah yah m·vee·ŋoh yah vee·ŋwah·jee.*
What do you recommend?	**Unapendekeza nini?** *Oo·nah·pen·deh·keh·zah nee·nee?*
I'd like a bottle/glass of red/white wine.	**Ningependa glasi ya mvinyo mwekundu/mweupe.** *Neen·geh·pen·dah glah·see yah m·vee·ŋo m·we·koon·doo/m·weh·oopeh.*

The house wine, please.	**Tafadhali nipe mvinyo wa nyumbani.** tah·fah·thah·lee nee·peh m·vee·ŋoh wah ŋoo·m·bah·nee.
Another bottle/glass, please.	**Tafadhali nipe chupa nyingine ya/glasi.** tah·fah·thah·lee nee·peh choo·pah yah/glah·see
I'd like a local beer.	**Ningependa bia ya kawaida.** neen·geh·pen·dah bee·ah yah kah·wah·ee·dah
Can I buy you a drink?	**Ungependa nikununulie kinywaji?** Oon·geh·pen·dah nee·koo·noo·noo·lee·eh kee·ŋwah·jee?
Cheers!	**Hongera!** hon·geh·rah!
A coffee/tea, please.	**Tafadhali nipe kahawa/chai.** tah·fah·thah·lee nee·pee kah·hah·wah/chah·ee
Black.	**Nyeusi.** Ŋe·oo·see
With...	**Na...** Nah
milk	**maziwa** mah·zee·wah
sugar	**sukari** soo·kah·ree
artificial sweetener	**kitu cha kutia utamu** kee·too chah koo·tee·ah uoo·tah·moo
A..., please.	**Nipe ..., tafadhali.** ne·peh..., tah·fah·thah·lee
juice	**juisi** joo·ee·see
soda [soft drink]	**soda** soh·dah
(sparkling/still)	**maji (yanayong'aa/matulivu)** Mah·jee (yah·nah·yoh·'ah/mah·too·lee·voo)
water	

Some local brews (**pombe**) that can be found in local villages are made from less conventional and even surprising ingredients. Look out for **moshi**, made of millet, maize or banana. Be careful as they are fairly potent concoctions!

Leisure Time

Sightseeing

Where's the tourist information office?	**Afisi ya habari ya utalii iko wapi?** *Ah•fee•see yah hah•bah•ree yah uoo•tah•lee ee•koh wa•pee*
What are the main sights?	**Sehemu muhimu za kutalii ziko wapi?** *Seh•heh•moo moo•hee•moo zah koo•tah•lee zee•koh wah•pee?*
Do you offer tours in English?	**Je unapeana huduma za kitalii kwa lugha ya Kiingereza?** *Jeh oo•nah•peh•ah•nah hoo•doo•mah zah kee•tah•lee kwah loo•ghah ya keen•geh•reh•zah*
Can I have a map/guide?	**Naweza kupata ramani/mwongozo?** *Nah•weh•zah koo•pah•tah rah•mah•nee/m•woh•n•goh•zoh*

> Wildlife parks and game reserves are numerous in East Africa and safaris are quite a magical experience. Many hotels can organize tours and excursions for you if you haven't already booked in advance.

Shopping

Where's the market/mall?	**Soko/supamaket iko wapi?** *Soh·koh/soo·pah·mah·keh·tee ee·koh wah·pee*
I'm just looking.	**Natazama tu.** *Nah·tah·zah·mah too*
Can you help me?	**Tafadhali nisaidie?** *tah·fah·thah·lee nee·sah·ee·dee·eh*
I'm being helped.	**Nasaidiwa.** *Nah·sah·ee·dee·wah*
How much?	**Ni ngapi?** *Nee n·gah·pee*
That one, please	**Ile, tafadhali.** *Ee·leh, tah·fah·t·hah·lee*
I'd like…	**Ningependa.** *neen·geh·pen·dah*
That's all.	**Tosha.** *Toh·shah*
Where can I pay?	**Nitalipia wapi?** *Nee·tah·lee·pee·ah wah·pee?*
I'll pay in cash/by credit card.	**Nitalipia kwa pesa taslimu/kadi ya mkopo.** *Nee·tah·lee·pee·ah kwah peh·sah tas·lee·moo/kah·dee yah m·koh·poh*
A receipt, please.	**Nipe risiti, tafadhali.** *Nee·peh ree·see·tee, tah·fah·thah·lee*

Sport & Leisure

When's the game?	**Mechi iko saa ngapi?** *Meh·chee ee·koh saah n·gah·pee?*
Where's…?	**… iko wapi?** *… ee·koh wah·pee?*
the beach	**ufuo** *oo·foo·oh*
the park	**bustani** *boos·tah·nee*
the pool	**kidimbwi cha kuogelea** *kee·deem·b·wee chah koo·ooh·geh·leh·ah*
Is it safe to swim here?	**Je, ni salama kuogelea hapa?** *Jeh,nee sah·lah·mah koo·oh·geh·leh·ah hah·pah?*
Can I hire clubs?	**Je, naweza kukodi vilabu?** *Jeh, nah·weh·zah koo·koh·dee vee·lah·boo?*
How much per hour/day?	**Pesa ngapi kwa saa/siku?** *peh·sah n·gah·pee kwah saah/see·koo?*
How far is it to…?	**Ni mbali wapi …?** *Nee m·bah·lee wah·pee …?*
Show me on the map, please.	**Tafadhali nionyeshe kwenye ramani.** *Tah·fah·thah·lee nee·ooh·ŋeh·sheh k·wen·ŋeh rah·mah·nee.*

Going Out

What's there to do at night?	**Usiku kuna shughuli gani?** *Oo·see·koo koo·nah shoo·goo·lee gah·nee?*
Do you have a program of events?	**Unayo ratiba ya matukio?** *Oo·nah·yoh rah·tee·bah yah mah·too·kee·oh?*
What's playing tonight?	**Ni nyimbo gani zitakazochezwa usiku huu?** *Nee ŋee·m·boh gah·nee zee·tah·kah·zoh·cheh·z·wah oo·see·koo hoo?*
Where's...?	**... iko wapi?** *... ee·koh wah·pee?*
the downtown area	**sehemu kuu ya mjini** *seh·heh·moo koo yah m·jee·nee*
the bar	**baa** *bah*
the dance club	**klabu ya densi** *klah·boo yah den·see*
Is this area safe at night?	**Je, sehemu hii ni salama usiku?** *Je·seh·heh·moo hee nee sah·lah·mah oo·see·koo?*

Traditional local dances are performed on special occasions. If you are lucky enough to come across one, you might see one of the following: **beni** (wedding dance), **bomu** (fancy dress dance prior to the wedding night), **unyago** (an initiation dance for girls) or a **ndege** or umbrella dance – women in colorful outfits, waving matching umbrellas sing and dance their way around town.

Baby Essentials

Do you have…?	**Je, una…?** *Jeh, oo•nah…?*
a baby bottle	**chupa ya mtoto**
	choo•pah yah m•toh•toh
baby food	**chakula cha mtoto**
	chah•koo•lah chah m•toh•toh
baby wipes	**vitambaa vya kumpangusa mtoto**
	vee•tah•m•bah v•yah koo•m•pan•goo•sah m•toh•toh
a car seat	**kiti cha gari**
	kee•tee chah gah•ree
a children's menu/	**menyu/chakula cha watoto**
portion	*meh•ŋoo/chah•koo•lah chah wah•toh•toh*
a child's seat/	**kiti cha mtoto/kiti cha juu**
highchair	*kee•tee chah m•toh•toh/kee•tee ch•ah joo*
a crib/cot	**kitanda cha mtoto**
	kee•tan•dah chah m•toh•toh
diapers [nappies]	**napi (nepi)**
	nah•pee (neh•pee)

formula	**maziwa ya unga**
	mah•zee•wah yah oon•gah
a pacifier [dummy]	**kisawazishi**
	kee•sah•wah•zee•shee
a playpen	**kalamu ya kuchezea**
	kah•lah•moo yah koo•cheh•zeh•ah
a stroller	**kiti cha magurudumu (kiti cha kusukumwa)**
[pushchair]	*kee tee chah mah•goo•roo•doo•moo(kee•tee chah koo•soo•koo•m•wah)*
Can I breastfeed the baby here?	**Je, naweza kumnyonyeshea mtoto hapa?**
	Jeh, nah•weh•zah koo•m•ŋoh•ŋeh•sheh•ah m•toh•toh hah•pah?
Where can I breastfeed/change the baby?	**Ni wapi ninapoweza kumnyonyeshea/ kumbadilishia mtoto?**
	Nee wah•pee nee•nah•weh•zah koo•m•ŋoh•ŋeh•sheh•ah/koo•m•bah•dee•lee•sh•ee•ah m•toh•toh

For Eating Out, see page 203.

Pharmacies are easy to come by in the big cities and the ones found in major hospitals are usually open 24 hours. Note that the smaller pharmacies often only sell medical goods but the bigger stores will usually also stock a full range of toiletries.

Disabled Travelers

Is there...?	**Je kuna...?**
	eh koo•nah...?
access for the disabled	**ufikiaji kwa walemavu**
	Oo•fee•kee•ah•jee kwah wah•leh•mah•voo
a wheelchair ramp	**mteremko wa gari la walemavu**
	m•teh•reh•m•koh wah gah•ree lah wah•leh•mah•voo
a disabled-accessible toilet	**choo cha walemavu**
	choh chah wah•leh•mah•voo
I need...	**Nahitaji...**
	Nah•hee•tah•jee...
assistance	**usaidizi**
	oo•sah•ee•dee•zee
an elevator [a lift]	**lifti**
	leef•tee
a ground-floor room	**chumba cha orofa ya chini**
	choo•m•bah chah oh roh•fah yah chee•nee
Please speak louder.	**Tafadhali ongeza sauti.**
	Tah•fah•thah•lee oon•geh•zah sah•oo•tee

Health & Emergencies

Emergencies

Help!	**Nisaidie!**	*Nee·sah·ee·dee·eh!*
Go away!	**Nenda huko!**	*Nen·dah hoo·koh!*
Stop, thief!	**Kamata, mwizi!**	*Kah·mah·tah, m·wee·zee!*
Get a doctor!	**Mlete daktari!**	*M·leh·teh dah·k·tah·ree!*
Fire!	**Moto!**	*Moh·toh*
I'm lost.	**Nimepotea.**	*Nee·meh·poh·teh·ah*
Can you help me?	**Unaweza kunisaidia?**	*Oo·nah·weh·zah· koo·nee·sah eeh·dee·ah?*
Call the police!	**Ita polisi!**	*Ee·tah poh·lee·see*
Where's the police station?	**Kituo cha polisi kiko wapi?**	*Kee·too·oh chah· poh·lee see kee·kho wah·pee?*
My child is missing.	**Mtoto wangu amepotea.**	*M·toh·toh wan·goo a·meh·poh·teh·ah*

YOU MAY HEAR...

Jaza fomu hii. *Jah·zah foh·moo hee*
Fill out this form.

Tafadhali nipe kitamulisho chako.
Tah·fah·thah·lee nee·peh kee·tah·m·boo·lee·shoh chah·koh
Your ID, please.

Tukio hili lilitendeka lini/wapi? *Too·kee·oh hee·lee lee·lee·teh·n·deh·kah wah·pee?*
When/Where did it happen?

Toa maelezo yake?
Toh·ah mah·eeh·leh·zoh yah·koh
What does he/she look like?

In an emergency, dial:
111 in Tanzania.
999 in Kenya and Uganda.

Health

I'm sick.	**Mimi ni mgonjwa.** *Mee·mee nee m·goh·n·j·wah*
I need an English-speaking doctor.	**Nahitaji daktari anayezungumza Kiingereza.** *Nah·hee·tah·jee dak·tah·ree a·nah·yeh·zoo·n·goo·m·zah kee·n·geh·reh·zah*
It hurts here.	**Nina maumivu hapa.** *nee·nah mah·oo·mee·voo hah·pah*
Where's the pharmacy?	**Kliniki iko wapi?** *Klee·nee·kee ee·koh wah·pee?*
I'm (...months) pregnant.	**Nina ujauzito wa (miezi...).** *nee·nah oo·jah·oo·zee·toh (mee·eh·zee)*
I'm on...	**Natumia ...** *Nah·too·mee·ah ...*
I'm allergic to antibiotics/penicillin.	**Nina uzio wa dawa ya kupunguza makali.** *Nee·nah oo·zee·oh wah dah·wah yah koo· poon·goo·zah mah·kah·lee*

Dictionary

a (no articles in Swahili)
acetaminophen [paracetamol]
  acetaminophen [paracetamol]
adaptor adapta
aid worker mhudumu wa jamii
and na
antiseptic cream krimu ya
  antiseptiki
aspirin aspirin
baby mtoto
a backpack mfuko wa kubeba
  mgongoni
bag mfuko/pochi
Band-Aid [plasters] plasta
bandages bendeji
battleground uwanja wa vita
bee nyuki
beige beji
bikini bikini
bird ndege
black nyeusi
bland (food) chakula
blue samawati
bottle opener kifungua chupa
bowl bakuli
boy mvulana
boyfriend rafiki wa kiume/mchumba
bra sindiria
brown kahawia/hudhurungi

camera kamera
can opener kifungua mkebe
cat paka
castle ngome
charger chajio
cigarettes sigara
cold baridi
comb (n) kichana
computer kompyuta/tarakilishi
condoms kondomu
contact lens solution lensi ya kutia
  machoni
corkscrew kizibuo
cup kikombe
dangerous hatari
deodorant marashi
diabetic mwenye kisukari
dog mbwa
doll mwanasesere
fly n kuruka
fork uma
girl msichana
girlfriend rafiki msichana/mchumba
glass glasi
good nzuri
gray majivu
great kubwa/kuu
Great Britain Uingereza
green kijani kibichi

a hairbrush burashi
hairspray kifukiza nywele
horse farasi
hot •enye joto
husband mume
ibuprofen ibuprofen
ice barafu
icy kibarafu
injection sindano
I'd like… ningependea
insect repellent kichukiza wadudu
Ireland Ailend
jeans suruali ya jeans
jungle pori
(steak) knife kisu
lactose laktosi
large kubwa
lighter epesi zaidi
lion simba
lotion [moisturizing cream] mafuta ya kulainisha
love upendo
matches mechi
medium wastani
monkey nyani
museum makavazi
my yangu
a nail file tupa ya kucha
napkin nepi
nurse muuguzi
or au/ama

orange chungwa
park bustani
partner mwenzi/mchumba
pen kalamu
pink waridi
plate sahani
purple zambarau
pyjamas pajama
rain mvua
a raincoat kabuti
a (disposable) ya (kutupwa)
razor wembe
razor blades nyembe
red nyekundu
safari safari
salty -a chumvi
sandals patipati
sanitary napkins [pads] taulo za hedhi
scissors makasi
shampoo shampuu
shoes viatu
small ndogo
snake nyoka
sneakers viatu vya michezo
snow theluji
soap sabuni
socks sokisi
spicy -enye viungo
spider buibui
spoon kijiko

a sweater fulana
stamp(s) stempu
suitcase mfuko wa nguo
sun jua
sunglasses miwani ya jua
sunscreen mafuta ya kujikinga jua
a sweatshirt shati ya michezo
a swimsuit vazi la kuogelea
a T·shirt tisheti
tampons kisodo
terrible adj mbaya sana
tie tai
tissues tishu
toilet paper karatasi ya choo
toothbrush brashi ya meno
toothpaste dawa ya meno
United States Marekani

Berlitz®

speaking your language

phrase book & dictionary
phrase book & CD

Available in: Arabic, Brazilian Portuguese*, Burmese*, Cantonese
Chinese, Croatian, Czech*, Danish*, Dutch, English, Filipino, Finnish*, French,
German, Greek, Hebrew*, Hindi*, Hungarian*, Indonesian, Italian, Japanese,
Korean, Latin American Spanish, Malay, Mandarin Chinese, Mexican Spanish,
Norwegian, Polish, Portuguese, Romanian*, Russian, Spanish, Swedish, Thai,
Turkish, Vietnamese
*Book only